Listen to Yourself for a Change

"We have the ability to solve most, if not all, of our problems in life if we know how."
— William W. Hewitt

The sound of your own voice is an incredibly powerful tool for speaking to and reprogramming your subconscious. Now, for the first time, you can select your own self-hypnosis script and record it yourself. *Self-Hypnosis for a Better Life* gives you the exact wording for 23 unique situations that can be successfully handled with self-hypnosis. Each script is complete and takes only 30 minutes to record. You simply read the script aloud into a tape recorder, then replay the finished tape back to yourself and reap the rewards of self-hypnosis!

Whether you want to eliminate negativity from your life, attract a special romantic partner, solve a problem, be more successful at work, or simply relax, you will find a number of tape scripts to suit your needs. Anyone can begin using this system in minutes. Become your own hypnotherapist as you design your self-improvement program and create the life you've always wanted.

About the Author

William W. Hewitt was a freelance writer, the author of eight books and other materials published by Llewellyn Publications. He spent more than thirty years as a professional writer and editor in the computer, nuclear power, manufacturing, and mining industries, and was professional member of the National Writers Association. He was a certified clinical hypnotherapist and a professional astrologer. He frequently lectured on hypnosis, mind power, self-improvement, metaphysics, and related subjects. After his retirement in 1994, he and his wife travelled extensively together, as a devoted couple enjoying their "golden years." William W. Hewitt passed from this life in November of 2001.

Self-Hypnosis

FOR A BETTER LIFE

William W. Hewitt

Llewellyn Publications
St. Paul, Minnesota

FIRST EDITION
Sixth Printing, 2005

Cover design by Anne Marie Garrison
Book design and editing by Astrid Sandell

Library of Congress Cataloging-in-Publication Data
Hewitt, William W. 1929-2001
    Self-hypnosis for a better life / William W. Hewitt. — 1st ed.
      p.   cm.
    ISBN 1-56718-358-1 (trade paper)
    1. Hypnotism. 2. Autogenic training. 3. Self-actualization
(Psychology)—Miscellanea. I. Title.
BF1152.H577 1997
154.7—dc21   97-25587
                                            CIP

Llewellyn Publications
A Division of Llewellyn Worldwide, Ltd.
P.O. Box 64383, Dept. K358-1
St. Paul, Minnesota 55164-0383, U.S.A.
www.llewellyn.com

Printed in the United States of America.

Other Books by William W. Hewitt

Hypnosis, 1986
Tea Leaf Reading, 1989
Astrology for Beginners, 1991
Bridges to Success & Fulfillment, 1993
The Art of Self-Talk, 1993 (out of print)
Psychic Development for Beginners, 1996
Hypnosis for Beginners, 1997

Audio Tapes

Become Smoke-Free through Self-Hypnosis
Psychic Workout through Self-Hypnosis
Relaxation and Stress Management through Self-Hypnosis
Your Perfect Weight through Self-Hypnosis

To

Nancy Mostad
and
Silver Ravenwolf

Table of Contents

●   ●   ●

1

Introduction

WE HAVE the ability to solve most, if not all, of our problems in life if we know how. Self-hypnosis is one tool that can help us solve our problems and create better lives for ourselves.

This book gives actual word-for-word self-hypnosis scripts for twenty three major problem-solving situations. Most of them will most likely apply to you at some point in your life.

All you need to do is make a cassette tape recording for whichever of the situations you think will help you. Make as many, or as few, recordings as you wish. Once you make them, you have them for life to use and reuse as you wish. Then you sit down in a comfortable position, turn on the tape, close your eyes, and allow the tape recording of your own voice to hypnotize you.

Simple, is it not?

You don't need hi-fi stereo with a wide-frequency band range for this. You simply record the tape scripts in your normal speaking voice, and any inexpensive recorder will do just fine for this. The same is true for the tapes. Purchase modestly priced ones. Expensive ones won't do any more for you. Each of the twenty three tape scripts in this book will require less than thirty minutes of recording time and will fit onto one side of a sixty-minute tape.

Several of the subjects have two tape scripts (Dreams, Phobia, World Peace). You can put one script on one side of a tape and the second on the reverse, thus having just one cassette for the complete subject of dreams, phobia, or world peace.

What Self-Hypnosis Is All About

Hypnosis is a method of boring your conscious mind so that it relaxes and stops thinking, much the same as when you go to bed at night just before you actually slip into sleep.

In hypnosis, your conscious mind becomes less active, but you remain awake. At this point, your subconscious mind is especially receptive to suggestions. It is your subconscious mind that responds to suggestions and causes those suggestions to manifest themselves in your life.

The subconscious mind is like an obedient servant—it just does what it is told to do. The subconscious mind doesn't think, reason, or rationalize, it only follows instructions. Conversely, your conscious mind does think, reason, and rationalize—and often argues against what you want. This is why the conscious mind needs to be relaxed and quieted so it won't argue against what you are instructing your subconscious mind to do.

This process is called *hypnosis*. Self-hypnosis means you hypnotize yourself. When someone else hypnotizes you, it is just called hypnosis. There is no difference in the process or results between self-hypnosis and hypnosis.

Through self-hypnosis, as described in this book and in my other hypnosis book, *Hypnosis for Beginners*, you are able to improve your life in any way you choose by directly instructing your subconscious mind in what you want to achieve. It is that simple.

Repetition and reinforcement of the suggestions are usually needed because hypnosis suggestion usually fades within a couple of weeks, and your subconscious mind needs to be told repeatedly what to do in order to convince it that is really what you want. This is because most people change their minds frequently, signaling the subconscious not to take them seriously.

However, once you remain consistent with the suggestions and convince your subconscious mind of what you want, watch out because it will become reality. Self-hypnosis is very powerful, so be sure of what you program your subconscious mind for, because you will get it.

The procedures in this book can enable you to work wonders in your life.

Making a Recording

At the beginning of each chapter I will first give a brief description of what the particular tape is about. Then I will have a heading titled "Tape Script." Record everything after the heading "Tape Script." In the script, if there are capitalized words, for example PAUSE 30 SECONDS, do not record those words. These are recording instructions for you, indicating that you should stop talking, but keep the tape running. When you read the scripts, you will see why these special instructions are occasionally needed. To effectively create and use a self-hypnosis tape, follow these simple instructions.

- Speak in your normal speaking voice.

- Speak at a pace that will be comfortable for you to listen to. Too fast, and you will have a difficult time keeping up with the tape when you listen to it. Too slow, and you might lose your concentration.

- Don't be concerned if you make minor speaking errors, just continue making the recording. Minor errors will not bother you when listening to the tape.

- Use either sixty-minute or ninety-minute tapes, whatever you have. Either works fine.

- Try to select a time and place for making the recording where you are not likely to be interrupted and where there is no annoying background noise. The quieter, the better.

- Take the phone off the hook while making a recording. One of Murphy's Laws is that "The phone will ring whenever you are making a self-hypnosis tape recording."

- Record the script in its entirety.

Listening to Your Recorded Tape

- Choose a time and place where you are not likely to be interrupted.

- Take the phone off the hook.

- Sit in a comfortable chair or recliner, or lie down if you wish. My personal preference is a straight-back armless chair. In some cases you definitely must be lying in bed (dreams, insomnia, etc.).

- Turn on your recorder, listen, and follow the instructions. Do what the tape tells you to do.

Now you are ready to make tapes and hypnotize yourself and solve problems and improve your life.

● ● ●

2

I Love...

EVERY DAY you are exposed to a barrage of negative words and actions. As a result, it becomes easy to slip into the habit of negative thinking yourself.

This negativism comes in simple everyday conversation. For example, if you ask someone how he has been, isn't the answer you almost always get, "Oh, I don't feel so bad!" Why must people compare their well-being to "bad" rather than to good? Wouldn't it be nicer to hear, "I feel good!" for an answer?

Aren't people always saying, "I don't like this or don't like that," whether it be a food, a place, or a person? It is always "don't like" instead of what they do like. Start paying attention to what you hear and you will see that my observation is accurate.

Television is another source of negativism. For instance, there is a commercial that goes something like this: "The flu season is here, so prepare yourself for when you get the flu by purchasing our product." They want you to get the flu so they can make more money. The truth is that there is no such thing as the flu season, and you will not necessarily catch the flu.

Newspapers give you a heavy dose of negativism, too. Nearly everything in the paper tells you what is wrong somewhere or with someone or some situation. You have to look long and hard to find an upbeat story in the newspaper.

This tape is designed to help you bring a heavy dose of the most powerful, positive energy that exists into your life—Love. Love will eradicate the effects of all the negative influences. Love will attract love and good fortune to you. Love enriches the lives of all it touches.

This tape and all the other love tapes in this series will help you to establish such a powerful, positive aura that all the negativism in the world will not be able to penetrate it.

You may use this tape as often as you wish, and I recommend that you use it frequently.

Love Tape Script

Close your eyes and take a deep, full breath and exhale completely, all the way to the bottom of your lungs. All out. Do it again now. Just relax and let it all out. One more time, and this time hold your breath when you have filled your lungs with clean, refreshing, relaxing air. Hold it in. Keep your eyes closed. Now let your breath out slowly and feel yourself relaxing all over.

I want you to imagine now that all your tensions, all your tightness, and all your fears and worries are draining away from the top of your head. Let it drain down through your face, down through your neck, through your shoulders, through your chest, your waist, your hips, your thighs, down through your knees, your calves, your ankles, your feet, and out your toes. All your tension, all your tightness, all your worries and fears are draining away now from the very tips of your toes, and you are relaxing more and more.

Focus your attention on your toes now and allow your toes to relax completely. Each toe is loose and heavy. Now let this relaxation flow into your feet, into your ankles, your calves, your knees. Feel it flowing into your thighs, into your hips, into your waist, flowing up into your chest now. Feel your breathing easier and deeper, more regular and more relaxed. Now let the deep relaxed feeling go into your shoulders, down your arms, into your upper arms, your forearms, and into your hands and fingers, and flowing back into your forearms, your upper arms, your shoulders. Flowing into your neck, over your face, your chin, your cheeks, even your ears are relaxed. Feel it flowing into your eyes and eyelids now. Your eyelids are so heavy and smooth. Flowing up into your eyebrows, over your forehead, over the top of your head, down the back of your head, and down the back of your neck.

A new heaviness is starting in your toes now. Twice as heavy as the first time. Imagine a heavy weight on each toe. Feel the heaviness deep and even more relaxed. And this heavy, deep feeling is going into your feet, your ankles, your calves, your knees, going into your thighs, your hips, into your waist. Flowing up into your chest now, relaxing your heart, relaxing your lungs, allowing your breathing to be more intense, more regular, more and more completely relaxed. Now the deep heavy feeling is flowing into your shoulders, and down your arms, your upper arms, your forearms, into your hands and fingers. And now flowing back through your forearms, your upper arms, into your shoulders, and into your neck. Flowing over your face, into your eyes, over your eyebrows, over your forehead, over the top of your head, down the back of your head and down the back of your neck.

And a new heaviness is starting now at the top of your head. Twice as heavy as before. Twice as heavy. Imagine a heavy weight on the very top of your head, soft and relaxed and heavy. Feel the heavy relaxation flowing down into your face and eyes now, down through your neck, your shoulders, flowing down through your chest, your waist, your hips, your thighs, your knees, into your calves, your ankles, your feet and toes. Deeply relaxed, loose and limp, and comfortable from the top of your head to the very tip of your toes.

I want you to imagine now that you are looking at a blackboard. On the blackboard imagine a circle. Into the circle we are going to place the letters of the alphabet in reverse order, and with each letter after you place it into the circle, you will erase it then from inside the circle and allow yourself to relax more and more deeply.

Picture the blackboard now. Picture the circle. Into the circle put the letter Z. Now erase the Z from inside the circle, and go deeper. Put Y into the circle, and erase it and go deeper. X, and erase it and go deeper still. W, and erase it. V, and erase it. U, and erase it. T, and erase it. S, and erase it. R, and erase it. Q, and erase it. P, and erase it. O, and erase it. N, and erase it. M, and erase it. L, and erase it. K, and erase it. J, and erase it. I, and erase it. H, and erase it. G, and erase it. F, and erase it. E, and erase it. D, and erase it. C, and erase it. B, and erase it. A, and erase it. Now erase the circle and forget about the blackboard. Just go on relaxing more and more deeply. Feel yourself sink into the chair, mind and body drifting deeper and deeper into relaxation, deeper with each breath.

As you breathe in, imagine that you are breathing in a pure, clean, odorless anesthesia. The anesthesia is flowing all throughout your body now. It is a warm, numb, tingling feeling, and the more you breathe in, the more you want to breathe in, and you allow your breathing to become even deeper now, bringing in more and more of this peaceful, relaxing, tranquil feeling. From now on until the end of this session, you will allow yourself to relax more and more completely with each breath you take.

I want you to imagine now that you are looking at a clear, blue summer sky. And in the sky, a sky-writing airplane is writing your first name in fluffy, white cloudlike letters. See your name floating fluffy, white, and cloudlike in a clear, blue sky. Now let your name just dissolve away. Let the winds just blow your name away into the blue. Forget about your name. Forget you even have a name. Names are not important. Just go on listening to my voice and allowing yourself to relax more deeply.

I want you to imagine now that you are standing on the top step of a heavy wooden staircase. Feel the carpet under your feet. The carpet can be any kind and color you wish . . . create it. Now extend your hand out and touch the railing. Feel the smooth polished wood of the railing under your hand. You are standing just ten steps up from the floor below. The stairs are curving very smoothly down to the floor below. In a moment we will walk down the stairs. With each step down you will allow yourself to relax even more deeply. By the time you reach the floor below you will be deeper than you have ever gone before. Take a step down now, down to the ninth step smoothly and easily. Feel yourself going deeper. Now down to eight, deeper still. Now down to seven . . . six . . . five . . . four . . . three . . . two . . . one. Now you are standing on the floor below. There is a door in front of you. Reach out and open the door. And from the room beyond the door a flood of light comes streaming out through the open doorway. Walk into the room, into the light through the open door. You are inside the room now, look around you. This is your room, and it can be anything you want it to be. Any size, any shape, any colors. You can have anything in this room that you want. You can add things, remove things, rearrange things. You can have any kind of furniture, fixtures, paintings, windows, carpets, or whatever you want because this is your place...your very own private inner place and you are free here. Free to create, free to be who you are. Free to do whatever you will, and the light that shines in this room is your light. Feel the light all around you, shining on the beautiful things in your room. Shining on you; feel the energy in the light. Let the light flow all through your body now. Going in through every pore in your skin. Filling you completely. Pushing away all doubt. Pushing out all fear and tension. You are filled with the light.

You are clear and radiant, glowing with the shining light in your room.

While you are standing in the light in your room you will have the opportunity to express your love to many people and about many things.

Now bring your mother into your room by mentally asking that she be present.

PAUSE 5 SECONDS

Now mentally repeat the following to your mother as I say it: "Mother, I do not pass judgment on you. I do not have the wisdom to pass judgment on anyone. You gave me life, Mother, and you always did the best you could. I love you for that, Mother, and I bless you and release you to your higher self."

I will stop talking now for thirty seconds while you express your love to your mother in your own way.

PAUSE 30 SECONDS

Now bring your father into your room.

PAUSE 5 SECONDS

Now mentally repeat the following to your father as I say it: "Father, I do not pass judgment on you. I do not have the wisdom to pass judgment on anyone. You gave me life, Father, and you always did the best you could. I love you for that, Father, and I bless you and release you to your higher self."

I will stop talking now for thirty seconds while you express your love to your father in your own way.

PAUSE 30 SECONDS

Now you will have the opportunity to bring other people of your choice into your room and express your love to them. They may be a spouse, brothers, sisters, friends, or even someone you have never met. You bring the people into your room by mentally calling out their names and greeting them with words such as "I love you and bless you and release you to your higher self" or use other words of your own choosing. I will stop talking for 90 seconds now while you do this. You may begin now.

PAUSE 90 SECONDS

Now mentally repeat the following to yourself as I say it: "I send my love to all those people who I have not yet sent it to."

PAUSE 5 SECONDS

You may now express your love about many other things. Repeat the following statements to yourself as I say them.

"I love life. I love all life, and I respect all life."

"I love all the creatures on this earth even though I don't necessarily care to be around some of them."

"I love all creatures because they are part of all creation just as I am, and they do their best to do what they must do to fill their role in life just as I do."

"I love my country even though it has its faults."

"I love myself in a quiet, self-appreciative way, and not in an egotistical, conceited way."

"I love myself even though I have faults."

"I love all the things I don't understand as well as all the things I do understand."

"Love is the driving force in my life."

Now take a deep breath and go deeper.

I will now stop talking for one minute while you meditate on love and express your love about anything you wish.

PAUSE 60 SECONDS

Now take a deep breath and go deeper.

You have created a powerful aura of love around yourself by your positive expression of love. This aura will attract love in many forms to you. Your life is greatly enriched as of this moment, and it will continue to be enriched the more you express love in your thoughts, words, deeds, and actions, and this is so.

Love is the driving force in your life.

Now take a deep breath and relax.

Every time you listen to this tape it makes you feel just wonderful. And each time you listen to this tape you will relax completely. You will go even deeper than you are now, and the suggestions will go deeper and deeper into your mind. By using this tape faithfully, you will bring more and more love into your life at every level of your life.

The next time you hear my voice on tape, you will allow yourself to relax ten times more deeply than you are now. And the suggestions I have given you will keep on going deeper and deeper and deeper into your mind.

In a few moments when you awaken yourself, you will feel very very relaxed, and you will be completely refreshed, alive, alert, full of energy, full of confidence, and full of love. You will feel simply marvelous. All you have to do to awaken is to count with me from one up to five and at the count of five, open your eyes, feeling relaxed, refreshed, alert, in very high spirits. Feeling very good indeed. 1 . . . 2 . . . 3 . . . 4 . . . 5.

● ● ●

3

Color Me Love

EVERYONE WANTS to be loved and to give love. Everyone has the right to love. This is a one-on-one romantic love tape and helps bring your true love into reality. It enables you to find and establish your true love partner. If you already have a specific person in mind, you can cement that relationship by using this tape. If you do not have a specific person in mind, this tape will enable you to be drawn to your true love or soul mate.

This tape works only "with harm to no one." Therefore, you cannot get your true love by causing harm to a third person. If your true love is currently bonded in a relationship with a third person, you can attract your true love to you, but it will work out in such a way that the third person is not harmed in any way. You must be willing to allow higher mind to work things out for you. Do not try to force the situation the way you think it should be or you will only bring disappointment to yourself.

You may use this tape as often as you wish. I recommend using it at least once a week and preferably every day until you and your true love find each other and become committed to each other.

Romantic Love
Tape Script

Close your eyes and take a nice deep, full breath and exhale completely, all the way to the bottom of your lungs. All out. Do it again now. Just relax and let it all out. One more time, and this time hold your breath when you have filled your lungs with clean, refreshing, relaxing air. Hold it in. Keep your eyes closed. Now let your breath out slowly and feel yourself relaxing all over.

I want you to imagine now that all your tensions, all your tightness, and all your fears and worries are draining away from the top of your head. Let it drain down through your face, down through your neck, through your shoulders, through your chest, your waist, your hips, your thighs, down through your knees, your calves, your ankles, your feet, and out your toes. All your tension, all your tightness, all your worries and fears are draining away now from the very tips of your toes, and you are relaxing more and more.

I want you to imagine now that I am placing on each of your knees a heavy bag of sand. Feel the sand pressing down on your knees. Your knees are growing heavier and more relaxed. In the sand is a very powerful numbing ingredient and the numbness is flowing down into your knees now. Your knees are growing numb and more numb under the sand. And the heavy, numb feeling is flowing down into your calves, into your ankles, into your feet and toes. Everything below your knees is numb and more numb from the sand.

And now the heavy, numb feeling is going up into your thighs, flowing into your hips, through your waist, and into your chest. It flows into your shoulders, and they grow numb and heavy. It flows down your arms, your upper arms, your forearms, into your hands and fingers. Flowing back now through your forearms, your upper arms, your shoulders, and into your neck. Over your face, your eyes. Flowing up to your eyebrows, your forehead, over the top of your head, down the back of your head, and down the back of your neck.

I want you to imagine now that you are looking at a blackboard. On the blackboard imagine a circle. Into the circle we are going to place the letters of the alphabet in reverse order, and with each letter after you place it into the circle, you will erase it then from inside the circle and allow yourself to relax more and more deeply.

Picture the blackboard now. Picture the circle. Into the circle put the letter Z. Now erase the Z from inside the circle, and go deeper. Put Y into the circle, and erase it and go deeper. X, and erase it and go deeper still. W, and erase it. V, and erase it. U, and erase it. T, and erase it. S, and erase it. R, and erase it. Q, and erase it. P, and erase it. O, and erase it. N, and erase it. M, and erase it. L, and erase it. K, and erase it. J, and erase it. I, and erase it. H, and erase it. G, and erase it. F, and erase it. E, and erase it. D, and erase it. C, and erase it. B, and erase it. A, and erase it. Now erase the circle and forget about the blackboard. Just go on relaxing more and more deeply. Feel yourself sink into the chair, mind and body drifting deeper and deeper into relaxation, deeper with each breath.

As you breathe in, imagine that you are breathing in a pure clean, odorless anesthesia. The anesthesia is flowing all throughout your body now. It is a warm, numb, tingling feeling, and the more you breathe in, the more you want to breathe in, and you allow your breathing to become even deeper now, bringing in more and more of this peaceful, relaxing, tranquil feeling. From now on until the end of this session, you will allow yourself to relax more and more completely with each breath you take.

I want you to imagine now that there are two full-length mirrors standing side by side in front of you. Visualize the mirrors. They are identical.

PAUSE 5 SECONDS

For the moment, the mirror on your left is blank.

Now see yourself in the mirror on your right. See yourself in this mirror.

PAUSE 5 SECONDS

Now repeat the following statement to yourself as I say it: "This mirror image of myself reflects what I offer to my true love."

Now put a red frame around this mirror. Red symbolizes attraction, passion, and depth of love.

PAUSE 2 SECONDS

Now allow the red color to flood over the entire mirror turning it and your image red.

PAUSE 5 SECONDS

Your image is now full of passion, attraction, and deep love for your true love. Now repeat the following statement to yourself as I say it: "I offer deep love and passion to my true love." Let the red frame and color disappear.

Now put a blue frame around this mirror. Blue symbolizes loyalty, warmth, faithfulness, and abiding friendship.

PAUSE 2 SECONDS

Now allow the blue color to flood over the entire mirror turning it and your image blue.

PAUSE 5 SECONDS

Your image is now full of loyalty, warmth, faithfulness, and abiding friendship for your true love. Repeat the following statement to yourself as I say it: "I offer loyalty, warmth, faithfulness, and abiding friendship to my true love." Let the blue frame and color disappear.

Now put a green frame around this mirror. Green symbolizes life, growth, and renewal.

PAUSE 2 SECONDS

Now allow the green color to flood over the entire mirror turning it and your image green.

PAUSE 5 SECONDS

Your image is now filled with ever-growing life and renewed dedication to your true love. Repeat the following statement to yourself as I say it: "I offer my life and ever-growing dedication to my true love." Let the green frame and color disappear.

Now put a purple frame around this mirror. Purple symbolizes spiritual oneness.

PAUSE 2 SECONDS

Now allow the purple color to flood over the entire mirror turning it and your image purple.

PAUSE 5 SECONDS

Your image is now filled with spiritual oneness with your true love. Repeat the following statement to yourself as I say it: "I offer my spirit to become one with my true love." Let the purple frame and color disappear.

Now put a white frame around this mirror. White symbolizes truth, compatibility, honesty, and integrity.

PAUSE 2 SECONDS

Now allow the white color to flood over the entire mirror turning it and your image a sparkling white.

PAUSE 5 SECONDS

Your image is now filled with truth, compatibility, honesty, and integrity toward your true love. Repeat the following statement to yourself as I say it: "I offer my truth, honesty, and integrity and total compatibility to my true love." Let the white frame and color disappear.

Now put a gold frame around this mirror. Gold symbolizes long-lasting value.

PAUSE 2 SECONDS

Now allow the gold color to flood over the entire mirror turning it and your image gold.

PAUSE 5 SECONDS

Your image is now filled with long-lasting value for your true love. Repeat the following statement to yourself as I say it: "I offer my long-lasting value to my true love." Let the gold frame remain around this mirror.

You have now created your love offering to your true love at a mental level. Now mentally repeat the following statement as I say it: "I offer all of my love to the person who is my true love and soul mate." It is now only a matter of time until it becomes manifested in the physical world.

Now turn your attention to the mirror on your left. This is the mirror for your true love or soul mate. If you already have a specific person in mind as your true love, create that person's image in the mirror now. See the image.

PAUSE 5 SECONDS

If you do not have a specific person in mind but you want to attract your true love, whomever it may be, then visualize a sign in the mirror that reads: "Image of my true love." If you should happen to get a person's image in the mirror, that is fine. Keep it there because it is your true love. If you do not get a person's image, that is fine, too, because your mind will reach out and contact your true love for you.

Now repeat the following statement to yourself as I say it: "This mirror reflects my true love and what I desire from my true love."

Now put a red frame around this mirror. Red symbolizes attraction, passion, and depth of love.

PAUSE 2 SECONDS

Now allow the red color to flood over the entire mirror turning it and your true love's image red.

PAUSE 5 SECONDS

Your true love's image is now full of passion, attraction, and deep love for you. Now repeat the following statement to yourself as I say it: "I desire deep love and passion from my true love." Let the red frame and color disappear.

Now put a blue frame around this mirror. Blue symbolizes loyalty, warmth, faithfulness, and abiding friendship.

PAUSE 2 SECONDS

Now allow the blue color to flood over the entire mirror, turning it and your true love's image blue.

PAUSE 5 SECONDS

Your true love's image is now full of loyalty, warmth, faithfulness, and abiding friendship for you. Repeat the following statement to yourself as I say it: "I desire loyalty, warmth, faithfulness, and abiding friendship from my true love." Let the blue frame and color disappear.

Now put a green frame around this mirror. Green symbolizes life, growth, and renewal.

PAUSE 2 SECONDS

Now allow the green color to flood over the entire mirror turning it and your true love's image green.

PAUSE 5 SECONDS

Your true love's image is now filled with ever-growing life and renewed dedication to you. Repeat the following statement to yourself as I say it: "I desire my true love's life and ever-growing dedication." Let the green frame and color disappear.

Now put a purple frame around this mirror. Purple symbolizes spiritual oneness.

PAUSE 2 SECONDS

Now allow the purple color to flood over the entire mirror turning it and your true love's image purple.

PAUSE 5 SECONDS

Your true love's image is now filled with spiritual one-ness with you. Repeat the following statement to your-self as I say it: "I desire my true love's spirit to become one with me." Let the purple frame and color disappear.

Now put a white frame around this mirror. White symbolizes truth, compatibility, honesty, and integrity.

PAUSE 2 SECONDS

Now allow the white color to flood over the entire mirror turning it and your true love's image a sparkling white.

PAUSE 5 SECONDS

Your true love's image is now filled with truth, com-patibility, honesty, and integrity toward you. Repeat the following statement to yourself as I say it: "I desire truth, honesty, integrity, and total compatibility from my true love." Let the white frame and color disappear.

Now put a gold frame around this mirror. Gold sym-bolizes long-lasting value.

PAUSE 2 SECONDS

Now allow the gold color to flood over the entire mirror turning it and your true love's image gold.

PAUSE 5 SECONDS

Your true love's image is now filled with long-lasting value for you. Repeat the following statement to yourself as I say it: "I desire long-lasting value from my true love." Let the gold frame remain around this mirror.

You have now created what you desire from your true love at a mental level. Now mentally repeat the follow-ing statement as I say it: "I desire all of the love from the person who is my true love and soul mate." It is now only a matter of time until it becomes manifested in the physical world.

Now study the two gold framed mirrors side by side. You on your right. Your true love on your left.

PAUSE 5 SECONDS

Now let the two mirrors blend together to create just one gold framed mirror that reflects both you and your true love side by side.

Repeat the following statement to yourself as I say it: "This is what I desire with harm to no one . . . my true love and I to find each other and become bonded in a long-lasting love that enriches both of our lives."

Now take a deep breath and relax as your mirror fades from view.

It is now an established fact. You and your true love are destined for each other in this current lifetime and with harm to no one. It is only a matter of time and patience until it all unfolds for you in the physical world, and this is so.

Take a deep breath and go deeper.

In a few moments you will awaken yourself. All you need to do to awaken is to count mentally with me as I count from 1 to 5. At the count of five, open your eyes and awaken. When you awaken you will feel fantastic, full of love, hope and optimism. 1 . . . 2 . . . 3 . . . 4 . . . 5. Open eyes, wide awake, and feeling just fantastic.

● ● ●

4

Let Me Sow Love

THIS TAPE is about love in the full scope of the meaning of the word *love*. This is not a romantic one-on-one love tape. The tape certainly covers one-on-one love, but goes much deeper and broader.

The powerful hypnotic suggestions in this tape can transform your life through the power of love into an extraordinary life of happiness and fulfillment.

Even if you listened to this tape only once in your entire life, your life would be enriched in some measure. Of course, you may listen to this tape as often as you wish, and I recommend that you use it frequently.

Transforming Love
Tape Script

Close your eyes and take a nice deep, full breath and exhale completely, all the way to the bottom of your lungs. All out. Do it again now. Just relax and let it all out. One more time, and this time hold your breath when you have filled your lungs with clean, refreshing, relaxing air. Hold it in. Keep your eyes closed. Now let your breath out slowly and feel yourself relaxing all over.

I want you to imagine now that all your tensions, all your tightness, and all your fears and worries are draining away from the top of your head. Let it drain down through your face, down through your neck, through your shoulders, through your chest, your waist, your hips, your thighs, down through your knees, your calves, your ankles, your feet, and out your toes. All your tension, all your tightness, all your worries and fears are draining away now from the very tips of your toes, and you are relaxing more and more.

I want you to imagine now that I am placing on each of your knees a heavy bag of sand. Feel the sand pressing down on your knees. Your knees are growing heavier and more relaxed. In the sand is a very powerful numbing ingredient and the numbness is flowing down into your knees now. Your knees are growing numb and more numb under the sand. And the heavy, numb feeling is flowing down into your calves, into your ankles, into your feet and toes. Everything below your knees is numb and more numb from the sand. And now the heavy, numb feeling is going up into your thighs, flowing into your hips, through your waist, and into your chest. It flows into your shoulders, and they grow numb and heavy. It flows down your arms, your upper arms, your forearms, into your hands and fingers. Flowing back now through your forearms, your upper arms, your shoulders, and into your neck. Over your face, your eyes. Flowing up to your eyebrows, your forehead, over the top of your head, down the back of your head, and down the back of your neck.

I want you to imagine now that you are looking at a blackboard. On the blackboard imagine a circle. Into the circle we are going to place the letters of the alphabet in reverse order, and with each letter after you place it into the circle, you will erase it then from inside the circle and allow yourself to relax more and more deeply.

Picture the blackboard now. Picture the circle. Into the circle put the letter Z. Now erase the Z from inside the circle, and go deeper. Put Y into the circle, and erase it and go deeper. X, and erase it and go deeper still. W, and erase it. V, and erase it. U, and erase it. T, and erase it. S, and erase it. R, and erase it. Q, and erase it. P, and erase it. O, and erase it. N, and erase it. M, and erase it. L, and erase it. K, and erase it. J, and erase it. I, and erase it. H, and erase it. G, and erase it. F, and erase it. E, and erase it. D, and erase it. C, and erase it. B, and erase it. A, and erase it. Now erase the circle and forget about the blackboard. Just go on relaxing more and more deeply. Feel yourself sink into the chair, mind and body drifting deeper and deeper into relaxation, deeper with each breath.

As you breathe in, imagine that you are breathing in a pure, clean, odorless anesthesia. The anesthesia is flowing all throughout your body now. It is a warm, numb, tingling feeling, and the more you breathe in, the more you want to breathe in, and you allow your breathing to become even deeper now, bringing in more and more of this peaceful, relaxing, tranquil feeling. From now on until the end of this session, you will allow yourself to relax more and more completely with each breath you take.

Find yourself lying on a soft, green meadow of grass with the bright sun overhead. Notice the flowers around your head. A gentle breeze ripples across your body. Notice the grass and flowers spring up to about a foot above your head. See how the breeze gently blows the blades of grass back and forth. Smell the fragrance of the flowers.

Now stand up and look to the north. See the majestic mountain at the end of this meadow. That is Love Mountain. Let's take a trip up Love Mountain. There is a stream on the right of you. Bend down and notice the cool water. Take a drink of this absolutely pure, clean, cool, refreshing water. Listen to the rush of the small rapids on this bubbly brook.

Since the stream seems to come from Love Mountain, let's follow it. Now we come upon a pond that is at the head of this stream. Notice how warm the water is here. Since at this level of mind we are all expert swimmers, let's go for a swim. Feel the warm sun. Feel the warm water surrounding your body as you quietly move through the water.

It is now time for us to continue up Love Mountain. As we climb, listen to the birds chirping. Smell the pine trees. Look at the rocks on the bank to our left. Once in a while, we can see the valley and our meadow down below on the right between the trees. We are halfway up the mountain now. Let's stop to rest on the rock to our right. Our meadow is in full view from here.

PAUSE 5 SECONDS

It is now time to continue up to the top of the mountain. Listen to the squirrels chatter in the trees above.

The breeze is blowing the smell of the small cedar trees to us as we near the top. We are on the top of Love Mountain now. There is a sturdy platform on the rim of the mountain overlooking a deep valley. A sign by the platform reads, "Stand here and ask for the twelve powers of love by calling down into the valley below."

Walk over and stand on the platform. Look down into the beautiful valley. This is the valley of love and in a few moments you will ask for your twelve powers of love and receive them. Take a few moments first to feel the tremendous power and harmony in this peaceful place. Give thanks in your own way for being here.

PAUSE 10 SECONDS

Now take a deep breath and go deeper within self.

You may now request your first power of love by mentally calling the following request as I say it: "Where there is hatred, let me sow love."

PAUSE 2 SECONDS

A voice from the cloud above you says, "It is done."

PAUSE 2 SECONDS

Now receive your second power by mentally calling down into the valley, "Where there is injury, let me sow pardon!"

PAUSE 2 SECONDS

The voice from the cloud above you says, "It is done."

PAUSE 2 SECONDS

Now receive your third power by mentally calling, "Where there is doubt, let me sow faith!"

PAUSE 2 SECONDS

The voice says, "It is done."

PAUSE 2 SECONDS

Now call out for your fourth power, "Where there is despair, let me sow hope."

PAUSE 2 SECONDS

The voice responds from the cloud, "It is done."

PAUSE 2 SECONDS

Call out for your fifth power of love, "Where there is darkness, let me sow light!"

PAUSE 2 SECONDS

The voice confirms, "It is done."

PAUSE 2 SECONDS

Call out for your sixth power, "Where there is sadness, let me sow joy!"

PAUSE 2 SECONDS

The voice responds, "It is done."

PAUSE 2 SECONDS

Call out for your seventh power, "Where there is contention, let me sow peace!"

PAUSE 2 SECONDS

The voice from the cloud says, "It is done."

PAUSE 2 SECONDS

Call out for your eighth power, "Where there is condemnation, let me sow forgiveness."

PAUSE 2 SECONDS

The voice affirms, "It is done."

PAUSE 2 SECONDS

Call out for your ninth power, "Where there is need, let me be a giving person!"

PAUSE 2 SECONDS

The voice says, "It is done."

PAUSE 2 SECONDS

Call out for your tenth power, "Where there is no love, let me give mine!"

PAUSE 2 SECONDS

The voice from the cloud responds, "It is done."

PAUSE 2 SECONDS

Call out for your eleventh power, "Where there is confusion and mistrust, let me sow understanding!"

PAUSE 2 SECONDS

The voice says, "It is done."

PAUSE 2 SECONDS

Call out for your twelfth power of love, "Where there is misfortune, let me sow consolation!"

PAUSE 2 SECONDS

The voice from the cloud declares, "It is done."

PAUSE 2 SECONDS

You have now received the twelve powers of love. Use them generously and you will in turn receive love and good fortune in tenfold measure in some aspect of your life, and this is so.

Now take a deep breath and go deeper.

I will now stop talking for one minute while you meditate on the beautiful, powerful experience you have just had.

PAUSE 60 SECONDS

Now it is time for us to leave the mountain of love and return to our meadow. You may return here whenever you wish. See the sun starting to set on the hills to the left. If we hurry, we can be off our mountain before it gets dark. Halfway down the mountain now, and we stop to rest on our rock again. We can watch the beginning of the sunset.

PAUSE 3 SECONDS

Start on down the mountain again. Hear the chirping of the small night animals. Passing our pond, we see the reflection of the sunset in its mirror surface. Our small stream is cool and refreshing as we pass along its side. Now we are back to our meadow. Lie down again in the tall grass.

Smell again the flowers' fragrance. Notice the grass and flowers return to their original height as our meadow and mountain now gently fade from view.

Now take a deep breath and relax.

The next time you hear my voice on tape, you will go ten times deeper than you are now, and the suggestions you receive then will go ten times deeper into every level of your mind.

Each time you listen to this tape, the quality and depth of love in your life will become more and more profound and evident. This tape enables you to enrich your life and the lives of all with whom you interact. The more you use this tape and practice using the powers it brings to you, the greater will be the enrichment in your life and the lives of others, and this is so.

Now take a deep breath and relax.

In a few moments when you awaken yourself, you will feel very, very relaxed, and you will be completely refreshed, alive, alert, full of energy, full of confidence. You will feel full of love for yourself and for everyone and everything. You will feel simply marvelous. All you have to do to awaken is to count with me from one up to five and at the count of five, open your eyes, feeling relaxed, refreshed, alert, in very high spirits. Feeling very good indeed. 1 . . . 2 . . . 3 . . . 4 . . . 5.

● ● ●

5

The Many Faces
of Love

LOVE IS the most powerful and most positive of all energies. Love is multi-dimensional. Most people think of love as the romantic relationship between two people who are "in love," or else of the relationship between family members. These things, of course, are certainly powerful evidence of love, but love embraces much more than this.

This tape enables you to embrace the various aspects of love and to make them a part of your life. This tape does much for your self-enrichment and can change your life for the better in every respect. This, and the other love tapes in this series, are designed to make you a powerful source and focal point for love. As such, no negativism can touch you.

You may listen to this tape as often as you wish, and I recommend you use it frequently.

Powerful Love
Tape Script

Close your eyes and take a deep, full breath and exhale completely, all the way to the bottom of your lungs. All out. Do it again now. Just relax and let it all out. One more time, and this time hold your breath when you have filled your lungs with clean, refreshing, relaxing air. Hold it in. Keep your eyes closed. Now let your breath out slowly and feel yourself relaxing all over.

Focus your attention on your knees now and relax everything below your knees. Relax your calves. Relax your ankles. Relax your feet. And relax your toes. Relax your toes. Everything below your knees is now loose and relaxed. Now relax your thighs as completely as you can. Let your thighs just droop limp and loose and heavy into the chair. Relax your hips and relax your waist. Now relax your chest as completely as you can. Allow your breathing to be easier and deeper, more regular and more relaxed. Relax your shoulders now. Let the muscles in your shoulders be heavy and loose. More and more completely relaxed. Relax your neck and throat. Let your head just droop as all the muscles in your neck just relax. Now relax your face as completely as you can. Allow your face to be smooth and loose, relaxed and easy, your jaws all loose and relaxed, your teeth are not quite touching. Everything smooth and loose and easy. Now relax as completely as you can all the little muscles around your eyelids. Feel your eyelids growing heavier and smoother. More and more deeply relaxed.

I want you to imagine now that all your tensions, all your tightness, and all your fears and worries are draining away from the top of your head. Let it drain down through your face, down through your neck, through your shoulders, through your chest, your waist, your hips, your thighs, down through your knees, your calves, your ankles, your feet, and out your toes. All your tension, all your tightness, all your worries and fears are draining away now from the very tips of your toes, and you are relaxing more and more.

We are going to do this relaxation exercise once again. This time I want you to allow yourself to relax completely. There is nothing to fear, you will always hear me, so just pull out all the stops and allow yourself to sink into perfect relaxation.

Focus your attention again on your knees and relax everything below your knees. Relax your calves, relax your ankles, relax your feet, and relax your toes. Now relax your thighs completely. Feel the deep and heavy relaxation flowing into your hips now. Feel it going up through your waist, flowing into your chest, to your shoulders, heavy and loose, completely relaxed. And now this heavy relaxed feeling is going into your neck and throat, all over your face. Your face is all smooth and loose, completely easy and relaxed, and the heavy relaxation is flowing into your eyes and eyelids now. Your eyelids are so heavy and so smooth. Ever more deeply relaxed.

I want you to imagine now that you are looking at a blackboard. And on the blackboard is a circle. Into the circle put the letter X. Now erase the X from inside the circle. And now erase the circle. Forget about the blackboard now as you just go on relaxing more and more deeply.

Focus your attention now on the very tip of your nose. Keep your attention gently focused on the tip of your nose until you reach a point where your entire attention is on my voice. And when you reach that point, you can forget about your nose and just go on listening to my voice and allowing yourself to relax more and more deeply. And as you keep your attention focused very gently on the tip of your nose I am going to take you down through four progressively deeper levels of relaxation.

I will label these levels with letters of the alphabet, and when you reach the first level, level A, you will be ten times more deeply relaxed than you are even now. And then from level A we will go down to level B, and when you reach level B you will be ten times again more deeply relaxed than you were before. And from level B we will go down even further, down to level C. And when you reach level C you will be ten times again more deeply relaxed than before. And then from level C we will go all the way down to the deepest level of relaxation, level D. And when you reach level D, you will be ten times again more deeply relaxed than before. You are drifting down now, two times deeper with each breath that you exhale. Two times deeper with each breath. Your hands and fingers are so relaxed and heavy, and they keep growing heavier. Feel the heaviness growing in your hands and fingers. Heavy . . . heavier . . . heavier still until now they are so heavy it is as though your hands and fingers were made of lead. And this deep relaxed, heavy feeling is flowing up through your forearms now. Feel it going up into your upper arms. Flowing through your shoulders, into your neck, over your face, over your eyes. Flowing up to your eyebrows, your forehead, over the top of your head. The deep relaxed, heavy feeling is flowing down the back of your head and down the back of your neck. You are now approaching level A.

You are on level A now and still going deeper. Five times deeper now with each breath that you exhale. Five times deeper with each breath. Your mind is so still and peaceful. You're not thinking of anything now. Too relaxed to think. Too comfortable to think. And this heavy relaxation in your mind is flowing into your face and eyes. It is flowing down through your neck and into your chest. Flowing down to your waist, down through your hips, your thighs, your knees, your calves, your ankles, your feet, and your toes. You are now approaching level B.

You are on level B now and still drifting deeper. Floating smoothly and gently into perfect relaxation. Your arms and legs are so relaxed and heavy they feel like logs. Your arms and legs are stiff and numb and heavy . . . simply immovable. Your arms and legs are like planks of wood. You are now approaching level C.

You are on level C now and still drifting down. Sinking into the chair. Sinking deeper and deeper into perfect relaxation. And as you go on drifting even deeper, I am going to count backwards from 15 to 1. Each number that I say will take you deeper and deeper still, and when I reach 1, you will be on level D. 15 . . . 14 . . . 13 . . . 12 . . . 11 . . . 10 . . . 9 . . . 8 . . . 7 . . . 6 . . .

5 . . . 4 . . . 3 . . . 2 . . . 1 . . . 1 . . . 1, so deep, so dreamy, so heavy, so misty.

You are now on level D and still drifting down. There is no limit now . . . no limit. Go on floating, drifting deeper and deeper into perfect relaxation, deeper with each breath.

As you continue to drift deeper and deeper into perfect relaxation, I offer the following suggestions for your benefit.

Of all the people you will ever know in your lifetime, you are the only one you will never leave or lose. To the questions of your life, you are the only answer. To the problems of your life, you are the only solution. Therefore, to achieve a life of love, harmony, peace, and fulfillment, you must create it. Love is the prime factor in achieving this kind of life. To get love, you must give it. Love needs to be directed inwardly toward self and externally toward others. And in directing love toward others, you show the deepest love and respect toward self. Love is much more than the romantic love toward a spouse or lover; much more than the love between family members or friends. Love has many faces, and it is important to integrate as many of love's faces into your life as you possibly can so that your life becomes eternally enriched. The suggestions that follow enable you to embrace the many faces of love. Repeat each of these suggestions to yourself with me as I say them:

I will show my love by being patient when I would rather be impatient.

I will show my love by persevering when it would be easier to give up.

I will show my love by smiling when I would rather complain.

I will show my love by saying "thank you" for all courtesies and kindnesses shown me no matter how small or trivial they seem to be.

I will show my love by lending a helping hand when I really don't have to or want to, such as holding a door open for someone, or helping clean up a mess that I didn't make, or taking a moment to be kind to a stranger who has a problem.

I will show my love by looking for opportunities to extend a pleasant word or action that helps someone else have a nicer day.

I will show my love by making a habit of saying "I love you" frequently to those who are close to me such as family members and dear friends.

I will show my love by giving my employer an honest day's work every day even when I would rather slack off.

I will show my love by being truthful when a little white lie would better suit my purpose.

I will show my love by conducting all my activities with integrity.

I will show my love by keeping my mouth shut when it would be more fun to gossip about someone.

I will show my love by keeping a secret when I would rather tell it.

I will show my love by saying a kind word when it would be easier to say an unkind word.

I will show my love by being courteous instead of being rude.

I will show my love by forgiving self and others instead of condemning.

I will show my love by being thoughtful of others instead of being inconsiderate.

I will show my love by extending friendship to those who are friendless and lonely.

I will show my love by getting involved instead of turning my back or making excuses.

I will show my love by thinking, saying, and practicing I CAN instead of I CAN'T.

I will show my love by demanding fairness and justice for myself and for all others.

I will show my love by being open-minded rather than being prejudiced.

I will show my love by doing at least one good deed every day that I really have no obligation to do, just because I want to and it makes me feel good.

I will show my love by controlling my temper when I would rather display my temper.

I will show my love by not taking any deliberate action that could pose a potential threat or harm to myself or to anyone else.

I will show my love by exercising prudence and sound judgment in all my actions.

I will show my love by not allowing myself to be misused, mistreated, mishandled, or made a fool of by anyone or any organization.

I will show my love by not misusing, mistreating, mishandling, or making a fool of anyone else.

Now, take a deep breath and go deeper.

You have just embraced some of the many faces of love.

Make these faces of love a living part of your life every day, and your life will take on a new dimension of joy and success, and this is so.

Now repeat the following suggestion to yourself as I say it, "I am making a commitment to myself to make the faces of love a part of my life more and more every day. I now realize that true love is a total dedication to the enrichment of all life . . . my life and the lives of all with whom I interact. I am dedicated to making love the dominant force in my life."

Every time you listen to this tape it makes you feel just wonderful. And each time you listen to this tape you will relax completely. You will go even deeper than you are now, and the suggestions will go deeper and deeper into your mind. By using this tape faithfully, you will bring more and more love into your life at every level of your life.

The next time you hear my voice on tape, you will allow yourself to relax ten times more deeply than you are now. And the suggestions I have given you will keep on going deeper and deeper and deeper into your mind.

In a few moments when you awaken yourself, you will feel very very relaxed, and you will be completely refreshed, alive, alert, full of energy, full of confidence, and full of love. You will feel simply marvelous. All you have to do to awaken is to count with me from one up to five and at the count of five, open your eyes, feeling relaxed, refreshed, alert, in very high spirits. Feeling very good indeed. 1 . . . 2 . . . 3 . . . 4 . . . 5.

●　●　●

6

Remember and Understand Your Dreams

THIS TAPE will help you to remember your dreams and to understand their meaning. Turn the tape on when you retire for the night and listen to it as you drift into sleep. The tape player will automatically shut off when it reaches the end of the tape.

Keep a pencil and paper near your bed because you may awaken in the middle of the night with the recollection of a dream or dreams. If so, write everything down while it is fresh; if you wait until later, you may forget some important details.

When you awaken in the morning write down everything you recall about your dreams. Typically, you may awaken in the night and recall a dream. Then you will go back to sleep and have more dreams which you will recall when you awaken in the morning. Be sure to carefully write everything down because that reinforces to your mind that you really are serious about remembering and understanding your dreams.

If the meaning of your dream does not immediately come to you when you are writing the dream down, mentally say,

"I want to understand the meaning of this dream!" The meaning may then come to you right away or in a flash sometime later.

When you remember a dream and understand it, say a mental "thank you" to your mind.

Remembering and understanding dreams is simply a matter of training your mind. At first you may get only fragmentary results, but eventually you will get excellent results if you persist. You should use this tape every night, or as often as you can, until you get your mind trained for results that satisfy you.

The other dream tape script in this book (in the next chapter) trains your mind to solve problems through your dreams. Therefore, it is wise to become adept at remembering and understanding before you can expect good results with the problem solving.

Dreams play a vital role in our mental and physical balance. Both a source of entertainment and of important information, dreams are one channel that our superconscious mind uses to communicate with us. Albert Einstein got his theory of relativity in his dreams.

Sometimes your dream can be interpreted literally. For example, you might dream of taking an airplane trip to Paris in the near future, and it turns out that that is exactly what will happen.

Other times you dream in symbols. For example, you might dream that a black bear is threatening to kill you. The bear might simply be symbolic of the black cigars that you smoke too many of. The dream is simply warning you that the cigars pose a hazard to your health.

Sometimes a dream is partially symbolic and partially literal, but in all cases, your mind can give you an accurate interpretation. If you learn to remember and understand your dreams you can open up new vistas of knowledge and experience.

Now just listen to this tape and follow the instructions. Do not fight sleep. If you wish to sleep while the tape is still playing, do so. The information will still be absorbed into your subconscious mind because your subconscious mind never sleeps.

Remembering Dreams Tape Script

Close your eyes and take a deep breath. Allow yourself to relax.

I want you to imagine now that all your tensions, all your tightness, and all your fears and worries are draining away from the top of your head. Let it drain down through your face, down through your neck, through your shoulders, through your chest, your waist, your hips, your thighs, down through your knees, your calves, your ankles, your feet, and out your toes. All your tension, all your tightness, all your worries and fears are draining away now from the very tips of your toes, and you are relaxing more and more.

I want you to imagine now that I am placing on each of your knees a heavy bag of sand. Feel the sand pressing down on your knees. Your knees are growing heavier and more relaxed. In the sand is a very powerful numbing ingredient and the numbness is flowing down into your knees now. Your knees are growing numb and more numb under the sand. And the heavy, numb feeling is flowing down into your calves, into your ankles, into your feet and toes. Everything below your knees is numb and more numb from the sand.

And now the heavy, numb feeling is going up into your thighs, flowing into your hips, through your waist, and into your chest. It flows into your shoulders, and they grow numb and heavy. It flows down your arms, your upper arms, your forearms, into your hands and fingers. Flowing back now through your forearms, your upper arms, your shoulders, and into your neck. Over your face, your eyes. Flowing up to your eyebrows, your forehead, over the top of your head, down the back of your head, and down the back of your neck.

As you breathe in, imagine that you are breathing in a pure, clean, odorless anesthesia. The anesthesia is flowing all throughout your body now. It is a warm, numb, tingling feeling, and the more you breathe in, the more you want to breathe in, and you allow your breathing to become even deeper now, bringing in more and more of this peaceful, relaxing, tranquil feeling. From now on until the end of this session, you will allow yourself to relax more and more completely with each breath you take.

Tonight you will experience a relaxing, restful night of sleep that is filled with dreams that are important to you. And when you awaken from your night's sleep you will remember all of your dreams in detail.

When you awaken you will write down all of the details of all the dreams that you remember. And your mind will furnish you with an awareness of the meaning of those dreams. You will also write down the meaning of the dreams.

Now repeat the following suggestions to yourself with me as I say them.

Tonight I desire to have dreams, and I will have dreams.

When I awaken I will remember my dreams, and I will write down what I remember.

I desire to understand the meaning of my dreams, and I will understand the meaning of my dreams.

I will write down the meanings of my dreams when I awaken.

Now relax and drift toward peaceful, restful sleep. As you drift deeper, I will count from ten down to one. Each number that I say will take you to an even deeper level of mind.

10, feel going deeper. 9, deeper still. 8, deeper and deeper. 7 . . . 6 . . . 5 . . . 4 . . . 3, deeper and deeper, 2 . . . 1.

Tonight as you sleep peacefully, you will have dreams.

You will remember and understand those dreams when you awaken. When you awaken, you will write down all the details of the dreams that you remember and you will also write down the meanings of those dreams.

If the dreams or their meanings do not come to you immediately, all you need to do is mentally say, "I want to remember the dreams I had last night and I want to understand their meaning."

The awareness of the dreams and their meaning may then come to you right away. Or they may come to you at various times throughout the day. Whenever you have an awareness, write it down.

Now repeat the following suggestions mentally to

yourself with me as I say them.

"Tonight I will dream and I will remember the dreams when I awaken."

"I will write down everything I remember about my dreams when I awaken."

"My mind will furnish me the meaning of my dreams and I will write that down also."

"I am training my mind to always remember my dreams and to always furnish me the meaning of my dreams."

"I am thankful to have such a marvelous mind."

"I am thankful that I have dreams that I can remember and that furnish me information."

Now I will count from five down to one. Each number will take you ten times deeper than before. 5, ten times deeper. 4, deeper, deeper, and deeper. 3, deeper still. 2, feel going still deeper. 1, very deep, very relaxed.

Tonight you will dream. When you awaken you will remember your dreams and will understand the meaning of them. You will write down everything you remember about your dreams and their meaning.

You are training your mind to bring your dreams and their meanings to your conscious awareness.

Now repeat the following suggestions mentally to yourself as I say them.

"I am training my mind to furnish me awareness and understanding of my dreams. My mind will obey and furnish me what I desire."

"Tonight I will dream. I will remember and understand my dreams when I awaken. I will write down everything I remember."

"I am thankful for this marvelous gift of dreams."

Now I will count backwards from 99. Just relax and let the numbers take you into a deep sleep where you will dream.

99 . . . 98 . . . 97 . . . 96 . . . 95 . . . (continue to record the countdown until you reach the count of 1 or the end of the tape, whichever comes first).

● ● ●

7

Using Your Dreams to Solve Problems

NOW THAT you have trained your mind to remember your dreams and to give you their meanings, you are ready to progress to the next step. This tape will train your mind to use your dreams to present you with the solutions to your problems.

The sequence for using your dreams for problem solving is this:

- First, relax and alter your state of consciousness—hypnotize yourself.

- Tell your mind that you want information to be given to you in dreams that will lead to the best solution of the problem that you have in mind.

- Mentally state the problem you wish to solve.

- Tell your mind you want to remember the dreams and to fully understand the information they contain.

- Go to sleep.

- When you awaken, write down everything you recall about your dreams. The solution to your problem may come to you immediately, or it may come later in a flash, or it may come by some other means.

- You may get the entire solution or you may get information that will lead to the solution.

When you remember the dream and understand the information or get a solution, say a mental "thank you" to your higher mind.

Now let us do all this in an altered state (self-hypnosis) training session as you retire for the night.

Listen to the tape and follow the instructions. Have the problem you wish to solve clearly in your mind.

Do not fight sleep. If you wish to sleep while the tape is still playing, do so. The information will still be absorbed into your subconscious mind. The tape will shut off automatically when it reaches the end of the tape.

Problem Solving with Dreams Tape Script

Close your eyes. Take a deep breath and allow yourself to relax.

I want you to imagine now that all your tensions, all your tightness, and all your fears and worries are draining away from the top of your head. Let it drain down through your face, down through your neck, through your shoulders, through your chest, your waist, your hips, your thighs, down through your knees, your calves, your ankles, your feet, and out your toes. All your tension, all your tightness, all your worries and fears are draining away now from the very tips of your toes, and you are relaxing more and more.

I want you to imagine now that I am placing on each

of your knees a heavy bag of sand. Feel the sand pressing down on your knees. Your knees are growing heavier and more relaxed. In the sand is a very powerful numbing ingredient and the numbness is flowing down into your knees now. Your knees are growing numb and more numb under the sand. And the heavy, numb feeling is flowing down into your calves, into your ankles, into your feet and toes. Everything below your knees is numb and more numb from the sand. And now the heavy, numb feeling is going up into your thighs, flowing into your hips, through your waist, and into your chest. It flows into your shoulders, and they grow numb and heavy. It flows down your arms, your upper arms, your forearms, into your hands and fingers. Flowing back now through your forearms, your upper arms, your shoulders, and into your neck. Over your face, your eyes. Flowing up to your eyebrows, your forehead, over the top of your head, down the back of your head, and down the back of your neck.

As you breathe in, imagine that you are breathing in a pure, clean, odorless anesthesia. The anesthesia is flowing all throughout your body now. It is a warm, numb, tingling feeling, and the more you breathe in, the more you want to breathe in, and you allow your breathing to become even deeper now, bringing in more and more of this peaceful, relaxing, tranquil feeling. From now on until the end of this session, you will allow yourself to relax more and more completely with each breath you take.

Tonight you will use your dreams to solve the problem you have in mind.

Repeat the following two suggestions to yourself mentally as I say them.

"I desire to find the best solution to the problem I have in mind."

"I desire my dreams tonight to furnish me with information that I will understand and that will lead to the solution of my problem."

Now I will stop talking for 60 seconds while you mentally define and review the problem you wish to find the best solution for in your dreams.

PAUSE 60 SECONDS

You have now stated the problem that you desire your dreams to solve.

I will now count from ten down to one. Each number I say will take you to a deeper level of relaxation.

10, feel going deeper. 9, deeper still. 8, deeper and deeper. 7 . . . 6 . . . 5 . . . 4 . . . 3 . . . deeper and deeper . . . 2 . . . 1.

Tonight as you sleep peacefully you will have dreams. These dreams will contain information that will lead to the solution to the problem you have in mind. When you awaken you will remember the dreams, and you will understand their meaning. You will understand the information you seek for the solution of your problem. You will carefully write down the dreams and their meaning for you to study and reflect on so you will have the solution you seek.

Repeat the following two suggestions mentally to yourself as I say them.

"Tonight I will dream and I will remember and understand my dreams when I awaken."

"My dreams tonight will furnish me with information I need to solve the problem I have in mind."

I will now stop talking for 30 seconds while you mentally review the problem you wish to have solved by your dreams.

PAUSE 30 SECONDS

The problem you have just mentally reviewed will be solved by your dreams tonight.

You will awaken with full recollection of your dreams and their meaning. You will write down everything you recall. You will understand the best solution to your problem when you study everything you have written down.

Now I will count from five down to one. Each number will take you ten times deeper than before. 5, ten times deeper. 4, deeper, deeper, and deeper. 3, deeper still. 2, feel going deeper. 1, very deep, very relaxed.

Repeat the following suggestions mentally to yourself as I say them.

"I am training my mind to provide me with solutions to my problems in my dreams while I sleep."

"I am thankful to have such a marvelous mind."

"I am thankful that I have dreams that I can remember and understand and that furnish me valuable information for solving problems."

Now I will stop talking for 15 seconds while you mentally state the problem that you desire to have solved in your dreams.

PAUSE 15 SECONDS

The best solution to the problem you have just defined will be given to you in your dreams tonight.

When you awaken, write down everything you recall about your dreams. Write down the meaning of the dreams. Then study what you have written and you will become aware of the information you need to solve your problem in the way that is best for you.

Now mentally repeat the following suggestions as I say them.

"Tonight I will dream dreams that will furnish me with the information I need to solve the problem I have in mind."

"I will write everything down when I awaken and I will understand everything I need to solve the problem."

"I am thankful for this marvelous gift of dreams."

Now I will count backwards from 99. Just relax and let the numbers take you into a deep sleep where you will dream dreams that contain the valuable information you seek.

99 . . . 98 . . . 97 . . . 96 . . . 95 . . . (continue to count down until you reach the count of 1 or the end of the tape, whichever comes first).

● ● ●

8

Affirmations for Adults

THIS TAPE is designed to be used at bedtime. As you drift into sleep, this tape programs many powerful, positive, constructive, helpful, successful suggestions into several levels of your subconscious mind so that you may enrich virtually every aspect of your life.

All miracles begin in the mind. This tape loads various levels of your mind with miracle-producing suggestions. Listen to the tape every night or as often as you possibly can and watch the changes in your life as you produce the miracles you want for the life you want. It really works, so please use it often.

The tape will shut off automatically at the end, so you do not need to try to stay awake to shut it off. Just let yourself drift into sleep while the tape plays. The tape's message will continue to go into your subconscious mind even if you are asleep.

Of course, you may also listen to this tape anytime you wish—not just at bedtime.

Affirmations for Adults
Tape Script

Close your eyes. Take a deep breath and allow yourself to relax.

I want you to imagine now that all your tensions, all your tightness, and all your fears and worries are draining away from the top of your head. Let it drain down through your face, down through your neck, through your shoulders, through your chest, your waist, your hips, your thighs, down through your knees, your calves, your ankles, your feet, and out your toes. All your tension, all your tightness, all your worries and fears are draining away now from the very tips of your toes, and you are relaxing more and more.

I want you to imagine now that I am placing on each of your knees a heavy bag of sand.

Feel the sand pressing down on your knees. Your knees are growing heavier and more relaxed. In the sand is a very powerful numbing ingredient and the numbness is flowing down into your knees now. Your knees are growing numb and more numb under the sand. And the heavy, numb feeling is flowing down into your calves, into your ankles, into your feet and toes. Everything below your knees is numb and more numb from the sand. And now the heavy, numb feeling is going up into your thighs, flowing into your hips, through your waist, and into your chest. It flows into your shoulders, and they grow numb and heavy. It flows down your arms, your upper arms, your forearms, into your hands and fingers. Flowing back now through your forearms, your upper arms, your shoulders, and into your neck. Over your face, your eyes. Flowing up to your eyebrows, your forehead, over the top of your head, down the back of your head, and down the back of your neck.

As you breathe in, imagine that you are breathing in a pure, clean, odorless anesthesia. The anesthesia is flowing all throughout your body now. It is a warm, numb, tingling feeling, and the more you breathe in, the more you want to breathe in, and you allow your breathing to become even deeper now, bringing in more and more of this peaceful, relaxing, tranquil feeling. From now on until the end of this session, you will allow yourself to relax more and more completely with each breath you take.

As you continue to go deeper and deeper with each breath you take I offer the following suggestions for your benefit.

Repeat the following three suggestions to yourself mentally as I say them.

Everyday in every way I am getting better, better, and better.

Positive thoughts bring me benefits and advantages I desire.

I am in full control of every aspect of my life.

I will now count backwards from ten to one. Each number I say will take you to an even deeper level of mind. 10, feel going deeper. 9, deeper still. 8, deeper and deeper. 7 . . . 6 . . . 5 . . . 4 . . . 3 . . . deeper and deeper . . . 2 . . . 1. You are now at a deeper level of mind. I offer the following suggestions for your benefit.

You are a good and worthwhile person. You are just as important as anyone else.

You have an excellent mind, and you are now learning to use more of your mind in a very special way to enrich your life.

You are in control of your own life, and whatever you choose to do you can do.

You will be completely successful, and you will enjoy your success.

Your aura radiates from you with the strength and colors that you decide by your mental, physical, and emotional condition.

You choose to be in such a positive, healthy, balanced state that your aura is powerful, clear, and brilliant with the beneficial energy you desire.

Now take a deep breath, and go deeper.

Repeat the following suggestions to yourself with me as I say them:

I am making a commitment to myself to enrich my life as I choose by using my mental powers more effectively. Using this self-hypnosis tape to program my mind with beneficial affirmations is one of the ways I am using my mental powers more effectively.

I am dedicated to creating a better life for myself and for all those with whom I interact.

I am creating a power center of love, success, and happiness within myself in order to attract benefit to me and to project benefit to others.

I am now going to count down from five to one. Each number will take you to a progressively deeper level of mind. 5, feel going deeper. 4, deeper and deeper. 3, deeper still. 2, deeper. 1, you are now at a very deep level of mind.

I offer the following suggestions for your benefit.

You can help maintain and promote good health by saying and thinking these words every day: "Every day in every way I am getting better, better, and better."

You are what you think. You are now commanding your mind to always direct you to lead your life in such a manner as to promote a long, healthy, happy life. And you will listen to and follow the beneficial dictates of your mind.

You will feel the natural freedom to love mentally, and you will feel free of fear and free of rejection.

When you engage in sexual activity with a consenting partner, you will become easily and quickly stimulated and aroused. You will thoroughly enjoy the sexual encounter, and you will bring pleasure to both yourself and your partner.

You are a beautiful, intelligent, and worthwhile person. And every day from now on you will become more completely the person you really want to be. You will be confident, relaxed, poised, charming, optimistic, and firm in your resolution to do what you want for your own happiness.

During your working hours you will feel relaxed and calm. Regardless of what happens, you will handle every situation in a relaxed, calm, and sensible manner free of tension.

I am now going to count from ten down to one. Mentally visualize each number as I say it, and when I reach one you will be at an even deeper level of mind than you are now.

10 . . . 9 . . . 8 . . . 7 . . . 6 . . . 5 . . . 4 . . . 3 . . . 2 . . . 1. You are now at an even deeper level of mind. As you continue to drift deeper and deeper with each breath I offer the following suggestions for your benefit.

Every day your will power becomes stronger and stronger.

You will not allow other people or situations to run your life. You are in control of your life, and that is the way you want it to be.

You will not allow yourself to be intimidated by anyone, anything, or any situation. Nothing can intimidate you if you don't allow it.

You have deep respect for your rights and for the rights of others. You realize that no one has the right to deprive you of your rights. You also realize that you do not have the right to deprive anyone else of their rights.

You desire to receive more love and to give more love because you know that love is the most powerful, beneficial force that exists.

You are committed to becoming more loving by being more patient, more understanding, more forgiving, more gentle in your words and actions, and more open and honest.

Now take a deep breath and go deeper.

Each time you hear my voice on this tape or on any other tape, you will go deeper than you have ever gone before, and the suggestions I give you will go deeper and deeper into your mind for your benefit, and this is so.

As you continue to drift deeper with each breath, I offer the following suggestions for your benefit.

You are a successful person, and you enjoy your success. Part of your success is your ability to manage your time efficiently. You plan your time and your projects, and you execute your plan promptly without allowing yourself to be distracted.

You are capable and efficient, and your creative mind knows what you can do. Your creative mind will find a way to lead you into the right circumstances and situations to best take advantage of your abilities.

You are a loving person, and you attract love and good fortune to you.

When you make love you do so gently but with enthusiasm, earnestly and with tenderness, and fervently for the mutual satisfaction of yourself and your consenting partner.

You are easily and healthily stimulated by sexual encounters with a consenting partner. You like to make love. You enjoy giving love and receiving love.

You are determined to live your life in the way that you decide is best for you. You realize that no one else has the right to decide what you should do or how you should live. You realize that the only restriction placed on you is that you do not have the right to do or say anything that deprives others of their rights.

You are now very relaxed, and you will continue to be more relaxed every day. You will always be relaxed and calm no matter what is happening around you. And anything that does happen, you can handle it in a relaxed, mature, and sensible manner. For you are in control now, and you are not intimidated by anyone, anything, or by any situation.

You will notice every day that your attitude is becoming more and more philosophical and free of serious concern about life's daily problems.

You like who you are, and you love the person you are now becoming.

You love life.

Every day you are becoming more and more the person you really want to be.

Every day you are becoming better, better, and better.

You are determined to achieve your goals and live your life the way you want.

You are a successful person, and you enjoy your success.

You will not give in to temptations that you know are contrary to your best interests. You will remain firm in all your resolutions.

You are a good, worthwhile and strong-willed person, and you like who you are.

Every day you become stronger and better in every way.

You have an excellent mind, and you will use it more effectively from now on every day.

You feel positive that everything in life will work out for you, and you feel good about it.

You can talk and think just as intelligently as anyone else, and you feel confident in all situations.

You will take people as they are. You will radiate warmth, and you will see people radiate it back.

You are the most important person in your world, and you will not allow anyone or anything take that dignity away from you.

You will not allow anyone or anything to determine how you are going to feel. You are in control, and you choose to feel happy, important, and worthy.

You feel the strength to stay away from any activity that is potentially harmful for you in any way.

You desire a long, healthy, happy life, and your mind will direct your activities and thought patterns so you will realize this goal.

Every day you will feel very relaxed, yet very alert.

You realize that fear is the only enemy a person can have, and you will not allow any fear to influence your life.

You will not put off doing the things you have to do.

You are now making a commitment to yourself to not put off until tomorrow what can and should be done today.

Never again will you be a slave to anything, to any person, or to any job. You are your own person, and you are in total control.

Yet, when you work you do so with integrity. You give a fair day's work for the money you earn.

You feel an intense interest in your work, and you feel a tremendous drive to perform to the best of your ability.

You are committed to your total success and to completely enjoying that success. You will allow your creative mind to lead you to that success.

You will achieve your success with harm to no one.

You are creating an aura that radiates love, integrity, honesty, and balance. This aura will attract to you all things good for your benefit, happiness, and success.

All these goals are now a reality at your mental and spiritual level. It is now only a matter of time, persistence, patience, practice, and perseverance until your goals become reality in the physical world, and this is so.

Now you will drift into a peaceful, relaxing sleep. While you sleep all the suggestions you received from this tape will continue to go deeper and deeper into your mind until they permeate every part of your mind.

When you awaken in the morning you will feel completely refreshed. You will feel full of confidence, happiness, and goodwill. As you go through your daily activities tomorrow you will begin to experience the benefits from the suggestions you have received tonight. Use this tape often and you will increase the frequency and depth of your benefits.

Now go to sleep.

● ● ●

9

Phobia and Fear Control

(Tape One)

TAPE ONE (the script in this chapter) and tape two (the script in the next chapter) contain self-hypnosis procedures to help you get rid of your fear or phobia. You will need to record and use both of these tape scripts as instructed in order to have a complete phobia and fear control program.

A phobia is a persistent, abnormal, or illogical fear of a specific thing or situation. Regardless of what your specific fear is, these two tape scripts will effectively deal with it because they approach the situation from a total fear perspective rather than dealing with only the specific fear symptoms themselves.

Let's discuss some facts about fear.

The fear you have experienced is completely your own creation. You were not born with a fear of height, or fear of open spaces, or closed spaces, or of being in an airplane, or in an elevator, or whatever your fear is. You created the fear that you now want to get rid of. Don't rationalize that someone else or some situation caused you to have the fear because that simply is not true. You chose to react to someone or to some situation in such a way as to create the fear.

It is your creation, and the first major step in resolving the problem is to accept responsibility for creating it.

Because you created the fear, you also have the power to get rid of it. The thing that is created can never be more powerful than the force that created it. Therefore, you, as the creator, are more powerful than the fear you created.

Herein lies your ability to get the fear out of your life completely if you really want to. These two self-hypnosis tape scripts guide you through a procedure for doing just that.

Secondly, recognize fear for what it really is—a cowardly, greedy runt. A coward attacks when your back is turned; it hangs back in the shadows where it can sneak up and take you unaware. This is the way fear gets to you—in a sneaky, cowardly fashion. Fear is greedy because it wants to rob you of your full enjoyment of life. You have a birthright to an enjoyable life, and this sneaky, cowardly, greedy runt wants to deprive you of that. Fear is a runt because it really is not big at all. It is only your emotional state that magnifies the runt into overgrown proportions.

We are now going to give this greedy runt a name. The name is GRUNT which stands for greedy runt. Whenever I use the word GRUNT I am referring to the specific fear that you are getting rid of. It makes no difference whether your phobia is agoraphobia, claustrophobia, acrophobia, necrophobia, or any other fear or phobia, the name of that fear is GRUNT. Start thinking right now of your unwanted fear as a GRUNT.

You will learn how to destroy the GRUNT in the self-hypnosis session in tape script two (next chapter).

Many factors come into play in creating a GRUNT. You become emotional. You have allowed yourself to become out of balance. You have allowed yourself to have a poor self-image. You have reacted poorly to stressful situations. You have allowed your self-confidence to weaken. You probably have learned to live with your GRUNT, thus making the GRUNT a habit.

The self-hypnosis session presented in tape one (this chapter) deals with relaxation, stress control, gaining self-confidence and putting yourself into balance. Tape two (next chapter) is the self-hypnosis session that enables you to destroy your GRUNT and establish a good self-image.

You may use either or both of these self-hypnosis sessions as often as you wish. I recommend that you listen to, and follow, both hypnosis sessions every day for seven consecutive days. First listen to session one, then session two each day. You may listen to session two as soon as you finish session one if you wish, or allow some time in between—it makes no difference. You may find it more comfortable to allow an hour or so between sessions so you can get up and move around and let your body get some exercise.

After one week, alternate the sessions for the next eight consecutive days. That is, do session one one day, session two the next day, and so forth.

You may find that you have destroyed GRUNT by this time. If so, you may discontinue or cut back on listening to the sessions if you wish. If GRUNT begins to show its greedy little presence again, start using the self-hypnosis sessions again until you are satisfied that GRUNT is gone.

In all cases, use your own judgment as to how often and when to use the sessions because you are the one dealing directly with GRUNT. These sessions give you the arsenal of weapons to eliminate GRUNT. So do it!

Phobia and Fear Control
Tape Script One

Close your eyes and take a deep, full breath and exhale completely, all the way to the bottom of your lungs. All out. Do it again now. Just relax and let it all out. One more time, and this time hold your breath when you have filled your lungs with clean, refreshing, relaxing air. Hold it in. Keep your eyes closed. Now let your breath out slowly and feel yourself relaxing all over.

Focus your attention on your knees now and relax everything below your knees. Relax your calves. Relax your ankles. Relax your feet. And relax your toes. Relax your toes. Everything below your knees is now loose and relaxed. Now relax your thighs as completely as you can. Let your thighs just droop limp and loose and heavy into the chair. Relax your hips and relax your waist. Now relax your chest as completely as you can. Allow your breathing to be easier and deeper, more regular and more relaxed. Relax your shoulders now. Let the muscles in your shoulders be heavy and loose. More and more completely relaxed. Relax your neck and throat. Let your head just droop as all the muscles in your neck just relax. Now relax your face as completely as you can. Allow your face to be smooth and loose, relaxed and easy, your jaws all loose and relaxed, your teeth not quite touching. Everything smooth and loose and easy. Now relax as completely as you can all the little muscles around your eyelids. Feel your eyelids growing heavier and smoother. More and more deeply relaxed.

I want you to imagine now that all your tensions, all your tightness, and all your fears and worries are draining away from the top of your head. Let it drain down through your face, down through your neck, through your shoulders, through your chest, your waist, your hips, your thighs, down through your knees, your calves, your ankles, your feet, and out your toes. All your tension, all your tightness, all your worries and fears are draining away now from the very tips of your toes, and you are relaxing more and more.

We are going to do this relaxation exercise again. This time I want you to allow yourself to relax even more fully and completely than you did the first time.

Focus your attention on your knees once again and relax everything below your knees. Relax your calves. Relax your ankles. Relax your feet, and relax your toes. And now relax your thighs even more completely. Allow your thighs to droop limp and heavy into the chair. Relax your hips and your waist. Feel the relaxation flowing into your chest now. Relaxing the vital organs within your chest, your heart, your lungs, allowing your breathing to be more intense, more regular, more and more completely relaxed. Now relax your shoulders even more. Feel your shoulders heavy and loose. More and more deeply relaxed. Relax your neck and throat. Relax your face even more. Feel your face all smooth and loose, completely easy and relaxed all over. And now relax even more all the little muscles around your eyelids. Feel your eyelids heavy and smooth, more and more deeply relaxed.

We are going to do this relaxation exercise once again. This time I want you to allow yourself to relax completely. There is nothing to fear, you will always hear me, so just pull out all the stops and allow yourself to sink into perfect relaxation.

Focus your attention again on your knees and relax everything below your knees. Relax your calves, relax your ankles, relax your feet, and relax your toes. Now relax your thighs completely. Feel the deep and heavy relaxation flowing into your hips now. Feel it going up through your waist, flowing into your chest, to your shoulders, heavy and loose, completely relaxed. And now this heavy relaxed feeling is going into your neck and throat, all over your face. Your face is all smooth and loose, completely easy and relaxed, and the heavy relaxation is flowing into your eyes and eyelids now. Your eyelids are so heavy and so smooth. Ever more deeply relaxed.

I want you to imagine now that you are looking at a blackboard. And on the blackboard is a circle. Into the circle put the letter X. Now erase the X from inside the circle. And now erase the circle. Forget about the blackboard now as you just go on relaxing more and more deeply.

Focus your attention now on the very tip of your nose. Keep your attention gently focused on the tip of your nose until you reach a point where your entire attention is on my voice. And when you reach that point, you can forget about your nose and just go on listening to my voice and allowing yourself to relax more and more deeply. And as you keep your attention focused very gently on the tip of your nose I am going to take you down through four progressively deeper levels of relaxation.

I will label these levels with letters of the alphabet, and when you reach the first level, level A, you will be ten times more deeply relaxed than you are even now. And then from level A we will go down to level B, and when you reach level B you will be ten times again more deeply relaxed than you were before. And from level B we will go down even further, down to level C.

And when you reach level C you will be ten times again more deeply relaxed than before. And then from level C we will go all the way down to the deepest level of relaxation, level D. And when you reach level D, you will be ten times again more deeply relaxed than before. You are drifting down now, two times deeper with each breath that you exhale. Two times deeper with each breath. Your hands and fingers are so relaxed and heavy, and they keep growing heavier. Feel the heaviness growing in your hands and fingers. Heavy . . . heavier . . . heavier still until now they are so heavy it is as though your hands and fingers were made of lead. And this deep relaxed, heavy feeling is flowing up through your forearms now. Feel it going up into your upper arms. Flowing through your shoulders, into your neck, over your face, over your eyes. Flowing up to your eyebrows, your forehead, over the top of your head. The deep relaxed, heavy feeling is flowing down the back of your head and down the back of your neck. You are now approaching level A.

You are on level A now and still going deeper. Five times deeper now with each breath that you exhale. Five times deeper with each breath. Your mind is so still and peaceful. You're not thinking of anything now. Too relaxed to think. Too comfortable to think. And this heavy relaxation in your mind is flowing into your face and eyes. It is flowing down through your neck and into your chest. Flowing down to your waist, down through your hips, your thighs, your knees, your calves, your ankles, your feet and your toes. You are now approaching level B.

You are on level B now and still drifting deeper. Floating smoothly and gently into perfect relaxation. Your arms and legs are so relaxed and heavy they feel like logs. Your arms and legs are stiff and numb and heavy . . . simply immovable. Your arms and legs are like planks of wood. You are now approaching level C.

You are on level C now and still drifting down. Sinking into the chair. Sinking deeper and deeper into perfect relaxation. And as you go on drifting even deeper, I am going to count backwards from 15 to 1. Each number that I say will take you deeper and deeper still, and when I reach 1 you will be on level D. 15, deeper, 14, deeper still, 13 . . . 12 . . . 11 . . . 10 . . . 9 . . . 8 . . . 7 . . . 6, let it all go now, 5 . . . 4 . . . 3 . . . 2 . . . 1 . . . 1 . . . 1, so deep, so dreamy, so heavy, so misty.

You are now on level D and still drifting down. There is no limit now . . . no limit. Go on floating, drifting deeper and deeper into perfect relaxation, deeper with each breath.

As you continue to drift deeper and deeper into perfect relaxation, I offer these suggestions for your benefit.

You are now becoming more relaxed, and you will continue to be more relaxed every day. You will always be relaxed and calm no matter what is happening around you. And anything that does happen you can handle it in a relaxed, mature, and sensible manner. For you are now learning to be more and more in control of your own life. You will no longer allow other people or events or fear to intimidate you or to cause you stress. You are in control, and you like it that way.

You will be calm, relaxed, confident, and in control at all times. You also have control over all your emotions.

You are learning to relax . . . to release all anxiety and relax and let go. For you are in control of all aspects of your life now. No longer will you allow anxiety, tension, or nervous energy to impede you. Every day you will notice yourself relaxing more. You will notice yourself becoming more calm and more in control than ever before.

You will notice every day that your attitude is becoming more and more philosophical and free of serious concern about life's daily problems.

Now repeat the following suggestions to yourself as I say them, "I am getting better, better, and better in every way, every day."

"I will always be relaxed and calm no matter what is happening. And anything that does happen, I will handle it in a sensible and mature manner."

"I feel positive that everything in my life will work out well for me, and I feel good about myself and the direction my life is now going in."

"Never again will I be a slave to fears of any kind. I am in control of my life, and that is the way I want it to be."

Now, take a deep breath and relax.

Picture yourself sitting on a large rock outcropping by the ocean with the sea about 20 feet below . . . notice the roar as the ocean rushes in and hits the rocks below you . . . smell the salt air as the wind gushes against your face . . . notice the contrast between your rocks and the beach.

Notice the sea gulls in the sky above . . . watch them dive for their dinner in the sea below . . . listen to their chatter as they return to the sky . . . notice the other birds around you . . . they show their appreciation for life in their smooth gliding and happy song.

Look behind you and you see a trail to your beach . . . walk down that trail to your beach below . . . the smooth path seems to indicate how many people have climbed down from your rock before you . . . these ageless rocks seem to reassure you of the beauty of life, and how, being in harmony with nature seems to give you grace . . . the stones and rocks seem to make a slight set of natural stairs about halfway down . . . now back to the sloping trail...the sand is warming up and is so inviting . . . the warm sun feels so good . . . take off your shoes and stockings. Leave them here on the sand where you can get them when you return. Now finish your walk to the beach barefooted . . . feel the warm sand squish up between your toes . . . feel the breeze warm you as you reach the beach . . . you are on wet sand now . . . feel its cool firmness under your feet . . . notice how differently this sand feels compared to the warm, dry sand you were on moments ago . . . look at the majestic expanse of ocean in front of you. It stretches as far as you can see. A gentle wave comes ashore and rushes past your feet. Feel how it tugs at you as it recedes back to the ocean. This ocean is the infinite sea of never-ending life and consciousness. Wade out into the water a short distance to where the water comes to your knees. This sea, of which you are a part, contains all the power you will ever need. Feel the power coming from the ocean floor up through your feet and legs bringing with it love and zest for life. Bringing with it courage and faith. Stand there and allow this priceless gift from the sea to fill your entire body. Flowing up through your legs. Into the trunk of your body. Flowing into your neck and head. You are filled from the sea of consciousness and life. You feel vibrant with love for life and for all. A powerful peace settles over you. Courage has filled every facet of your being. You know you can handle anything in a sensible and beneficial manner. You fear nothing at all. You have no fear, and this is so. Tremendous faith races through you. There is no room for doubt, and you have no doubts. You have received faith, courage, power, and zest for life from this infinite source of goodness. Now walk back to the beach to the point where an occasional wave washes past your ankles. Bend down and write in the wet sand with your finger this message, "I love." Now under your "I love" message write the names of all those special people you wish to send love. Be sure to include your own name. I will stop talking while you write the names.

PAUSE 60 SECONDS

If you have not yet written your own name, do so quickly now. Now a wave from the sea of consciousness washes up over your message and past your ankles. The wave recedes, washing the beach clean. Your love message has been carried into the sea of universal consciousness where it has become reality. Bend down and write in the wet sand once more. This time write "I forgive" followed by your own name first, and then the names of all whom you believe have wronged you in some way. I will give you time now to do this.

PAUSE 60 SECONDS

Now at the end of your list write these words: "AND ALL OTHERS." Now another wave from the sea of infinite consciousness washes over your message and past your ankles. When the wave retreats to the sea it takes with it your message of forgiveness which has now become reality. You have now purged yourself of guilt, blame, and animosity. You have filled your life with love, courage, faith, and zest. You are in balance and in harmony with all. You are now ready to serve with integrity and success.

Now stand up and face the sea of life once again. Turn your head to the right and look up the beach . . . that is the direction of the past. There is an open door a short distance from you in that direction. Now turn your head around to your left and look up the beach in that direction . . . that is the direction of the future. There is a closed door a short distance from you in that direction.

Now look back toward the sea of life and consciousness. The breeze from the ocean brings you the awareness of what you must do now . . . you must close the door to the past and open the door to the future. So turn to your right now and walk to the open door of the past. The door has a big sign on it that reads THE PAST. There is a key hanging on a nail on the doorjamb. Take the key into your hand. Take one brief look through the open doorway . . . you see all the mistakes, grief, and wasted energies that once were a part of your life. Now pull the door firmly shut and lock it with the key. Now turn and throw the key far out into the sea, never to be recovered. You have closed and locked the door to all negative aspects of your past. Never again will you need to look through that door. What occurred behind that door is over forever. It is not you now in this present moment. If you ever decide to go through the door to your past in order to regress into past life experiences you will be able to do so with no problem. What you have just done now in locking the door to the past is to prevent all negative aspects of the past from invading your present and influencing your present life in a negative way.

Now turn around and walk up the beach to the closed door of the future...as you approach the door you notice a sign on the door that says THE FUTURE. There is a golden key hanging from the doorjamb. Take the key in your hand and unlock the door. Open the door wide and look through. You see yourself as you really want to be and as you are now becoming. You see brightness and light. You see success and harmony. Take a few moments to get a brief glimpse of your future.

PAUSE 10 SECONDS

You have now opened the door to your future . . . to new hope . . . to new achievement and understanding . . . to a new you. Feel good about yourself.

Now walk back toward where you left your shoes and stockings. Pick up that sea shell you see lying in the sand just ahead of you and put it to your ear and listen to the message from the shell.

PAUSE 5 SECONDS

Now turn and look at the sea once more and say "good-bye" . . . it is time to return to put on your shoes and stockings...go back up the stairs of life . . . to the top of the rock. You have the love and excitement of life drawn up from the sea within you now . . . say a special thanks to those people who have been thoughtful to you as your sea fades from view.

You have just experienced an altered state of consciousness that put you into balance mentally and spiritually. You have been given this valuable tool to use to enrich your life. Use it every day to design your life the way you want it to be. At this moment you are making a commitment to yourself. A commitment to keep yourself free of all negativism from now on and to make your life a positive, happy, fulfilling experience that is completely free from fear. The choice is yours alone to do or not to do. For you are in control now. And whatever you choose to do, you can do. Whatever you set your own mind to achieve, you can and you will achieve it. You will be completely successful and you will enjoy your success. You will be completely free of fear. You will enjoy being the positive, worthwhile person you really want to be more and more every day.

Now take a deep breath and go deeper.

Every time you listen to this tape it makes you feel just wonderful. And each time you listen to this tape you will relax completely. You will go even deeper than you are now, and the suggestions will go deeper and deeper into your mind. By using this tape faithfully every day, you will have perfect control over your life. You can dissolve away any fear. You can dissolve away any tension. You can dissolve away any feelings of inadequacy. You will keep on performing better and better, and you will keep on feeling good every single day. You are an intelligent and worthwhile person. And every day from now on you will become more completely the person you really want to be. You will be confident, relaxed, poised, charming, optimistic, and firm in your resolution to do what you want for your own happiness. You will be completely free of fear, and this is so.

The next time you hear my voice on tape, you will allow yourself to relax ten times more deeply than you are now. And the suggestions I have given you will keep on going deeper and deeper and deeper into your mind.

In a few moments when you awaken yourself, you will feel very very relaxed, and you will be completely refreshed, alive, alert, full of energy, full of confidence. You will feel simply marvelous. All you have to do to awaken is to count with me from one up to five and at the count of five, open your eyes, feeling relaxed, refreshed, alert, in very high spirits. Feeling very good indeed. 1 . . . 2 . . . 3 . . . 4 . . . 5.

• • •

Phobia and Fear Control

(Tape Two)

10

IF YOU have not yet read the preceding chapter, Phobia and Fear Control (Tape One) please do so now before continuing with this chapter as it contains prerequisite information.

This chapter (tape two) deals with your specific fear so you can be free from it from now on.

Get a pen or pencil and paper and write on the paper the specific fear that you wish to get rid of. You don't need to describe all the aspects of the fear. Just identify it. For example: fear of heights, agoraphobia, fear of cats, fear of the dark, fear of being alone, or whatever is the correct identity of your fear.

Keep your paper within reach because you will need to open your eyes briefly and read it during this self-hypnosis session.

During this self-hypnosis session you will be required to do a physical action. You will be directed to hold out one of your hands, palm up, and point at that palm with the index finger of your other hand while you snap the fingers of the hand you are pointing with. You must actually do it physically. It is not sufficient to just think about it in your mind—you must actually do it.

This tape script will program this physical action into your mind as a method of destroying your fear. You will see how this works when you read the self-hypnosis script. This is a vitally important, tried and proven method that works. The idea is that whenever you feel your fear begin to attack, you can place the fear in the palm of one hand while you point a finger and snap your fingers with the other. Each snap reduces the fear fifty percent. By repeated snapping, you actually make it disappear.

Some people are unable to snap their fingers. If that is the case with you, then you must say the word "GONE" out loud instead of snapping your fingers. The details of how you do this will follow shortly in the hypnosis session.

The important thing is that you must actually do it physically. If you are out in a crowd and your fear begins to attack, you must right then and there put the fear into your hand and point and snap at it (or point and say GONE out loud).

You must not be concerned about "what people might think" if they see you. If you are not committed enough to do this simple physical action whenever and wherever it becomes necessary, then you are not committed to getting rid of your fear.

From this moment on, I am going to refer to your fear as GRUNT just as I discussed in the preceding chapter.

Make up your mind now that you are going to shrink GRUNT with your finger pointing and snapping (or saying GONE out loud) whenever GRUNT rears his unwelcome presence. If you are unwilling to make this commitment, then you really are not serious about getting rid of GRUNT.

For anyone with a physical limitation that prevents the use of one hand, place the fear in the functioning hand and say GONE out loud while staring at the palm of the hand. If neither hand can be used, place the fear on your lap, stare, and say GONE. In other words, if you have a physical limitation, use your creative imagination to revise the tape script so that it will work with your limitation.

If you do not have any physical limitations, then you must follow this script as it is given. No exceptions. No easy way out of taking the required physical actions demanded by the script.

Phobia and Fear Control
Tape Script Two

Close your eyes and take a deep, full breath and exhale completely, all the way to the bottom of your lungs. All out. Do it again now. Just relax and let it all out. One more time, and this time hold your breath when you have filled your lungs with clean, refreshing, relaxing air. Hold it in. Keep your eyes closed. Now let your breath out slowly and feel yourself relaxing all over.

I want you to imagine now that all your tensions, all your tightness, and all your fears and worries are draining away from the top of your head. Let it drain down through your face, down through your neck, through your shoulders, through your chest, your waist, your hips, your thighs, down through your knees, your calves, your ankles, your feet, and out your toes. All your tension, all your tightness, all your worries and fears are draining away now from the very tips of your toes, and you are relaxing more and more.

Focus your attention on your toes now and allow your toes to relax completely. Each toe is loose and heavy. Now let this relaxation flow into your feet, into your ankles, your calves, your knees. Feel it flowing into your thighs, into your hips, into your waist, flowing up into your chest now. Feel your breathing easier and deeper, more regular and more relaxed. Now let the deep relaxed feeling go into your shoulders, down your arms, into your upper arms, your forearms, and into your hands and fingers, and flowing back into your forearms, your upper arms, your shoulders. Flowing into your neck, over your face, your chin, your cheeks, even your ears are relaxed. Feel it flowing into your eyes and eyelids now. Your eyelids are so heavy and smooth. Flowing up into your eyebrows, over your forehead, over the top of your head, down the back of your head, and down the back of your neck.

A new heaviness is starting in your toes now. Twice as heavy as the first time. Imagine a heavy weight on each toe. Feel the heaviness deep and even more relaxed. And this heavy, deep feeling is going into your feet, your ankles, your calves, your knees, going into your thighs, your hips, into your waist. Flowing up into your chest now, relaxing your heart, relaxing your lungs, allowing your breathing to be more intense, more regular, more and more completely relaxed. Now the deep heavy feeling is flowing into your shoulders, and down your arms, your upper arms, your forearms, into your hands and fingers. And now flowing back through your forearms, your upper arms, into your shoulders and into your neck. Flowing over your face, into your eyes, over your eyebrows, over your forehead, over the top of your head, down the back of your head and down the back of your neck.

And a new heaviness is starting now at the top of your head. Twice as heavy as before. Twice as heavy. Imagine a heavy weight on the very top of your head, soft and relaxed and heavy. Feel the heavy relaxation flowing down into your face and eyes now, down through your neck, your shoulders, flowing down through your chest, your waist, your hips, your thighs, your knees, into your calves, your ankles, your feet and toes. Deeply relaxed, loose and limp, and comfortable from the top of your head to the very tip of your toes.

I want you to imagine now that you are looking at a blackboard. On the blackboard imagine a circle. Into the circle we are going to place the letters of the alphabet in reverse order, and with each letter after you place it into the circle, you will erase it then from inside the circle and allow yourself to relax more and more deeply.

Picture the blackboard now. Picture the circle. Into the circle put the letter Z. Now erase the Z from inside the circle, and go deeper. Put Y into the circle, and erase it and go deeper. X, and erase it and go deeper still. W, and erase it. V, and erase it. U, and erase it. T, and erase it. S, and erase it. R, and erase it. Q, and erase it. P, and erase it. O, and erase it. N, and erase it. M, and erase it. L, and erase it. K, and erase it. J, and erase it. I, and erase it. H, and erase it. G, and erase it. F and erase it. E, and erase it. D, and erase it. C, and erase it. B, and erase it. A, and erase it. Now erase the circle and forget about the blackboard. Just go on relaxing more and more deeply. Feel yourself sink into the chair, mind and body drifting deeper and deeper into relaxation, deeper with each breath.

As you breathe in, imagine that you are breathing in a pure, clean, odorless anesthesia. The anesthesia is flowing all throughout your body now. It is a warm, numb, tingling feeling, and the more you breathe in, the more you want to breathe in, and you allow your breathing to become even deeper now, bringing in more and more of this peaceful, relaxing, tranquil feeling. From now on until the end of this session, you will allow yourself to relax more and more completely with each breath you take.

I want you to imagine now that you are looking at a clear, blue summer sky. And in the sky, a sky-writing airplane is writing your first name in fluffy, white cloudlike letters. See your name floating fluffy, white, and cloudlike in a clear, blue sky. Now let your name just dissolve away. Let the winds just blow your name away into the blue. Forget about your name. Forget you even have a name. Names are not important. Just go on listening to my voice and allowing yourself to relax more deeply.

I want you to imagine now that you are standing on the top step of a heavy wooden staircase. Feel the carpet under your feet. The carpet can be any kind and color you wish . . . create it. Now extend your hand out and touch the railing.

Feel the smooth polished wood of the railing under your hand. You are standing just ten steps up from the floor below. The stairs are curving very smoothly down to the floor below. In a moment we will walk down the stairs. With each step down you will allow yourself to relax even more deeply. By the time you reach the floor below you will be deeper than you have ever gone before. Take a step down now, down to the ninth step smoothly and easily. Feel yourself going deeper. Now down to eight, deeper still. Now down to seven . . . six . . . five . . . four . . . three . . . two . . . one. Now you are standing on the floor below. There is a door in front of you. Reach out and open the door. And from the room beyond the door a flood of light comes streaming out through the open doorway. Walk into the room, into the light through the open door. You are inside the room now, look around you. This is your room, and it can be anything you want it to be. Any size, any shape, any colors. You can have anything in this room that you want. You can add things, remove things, rearrange things. You can have any kind of furniture, fixtures, paintings, windows, carpets, or whatever you want because this is your place . . . your very own private inner place and you are free here. Free to create, free to be who you are. Free to do whatever you will, and the light that shines in this room is your light. Feel the light all around you, shining on the beautiful things in your room. Shining on you; feel the energy in the light. Let the light flow all through your body now. Going in through every pore in your skin. Filling you completely. Pushing away all doubt. Pushing out all fear and tension. You are filled with the light. You are clear and radiant, glowing with the shining light in your room.

While you are standing in the light in your room, I want you to open your eyes and to read the fear you have written on your paper. When you open your eyes you will not awaken. You will not awaken. I will stop talking for fifteen seconds while you read the fear you have identified on your paper. Now open your eyes and read your paper.

PAUSE 15 SECONDS

Now close your eyes. Take a deep breath and go deeper. You have now identified your fear to your mind. Now we are going to give a name to the fear you wrote on your paper. We are going to name that fear as GRUNT. Repeat the following to yourself as I say it: "I have given my fear the name GRUNT. GRUNT is a greedy runt that I want to be completely rid of, and I intend to get rid of GRUNT now."

PAUSE 2 SECONDS

I now want you to imagine what GRUNT looks like. Give GRUNT a specific appearance. Perhaps little, beady green eyes. A sneaky look on its face. Or whatever. I will now stop talking for one minute now while you create the image of your GRUNT.

PAUSE 60 SECONDS

Now you know exactly what GRUNT looks like. Now physically hold out one of your hands palm up and place GRUNT into your hand. Keep your eyes closed. See how puny and weak and harmless GRUNT is here in the bright light of your room. You can hold GRUNT easily in your hand.

Now take your other hand and point your finger at GRUNT.

In a moment I am going to ask you to physically snap your fingers and watch GRUNT shrink to fifty percent of its size. If you are unable to snap your fingers when I say "snap" you may say "gone" out loud.

Ready now? Snap your fingers once and notice GRUNT shrink to fifty percent of its size.

PAUSE 3 SECONDS

Snap again, and watch GRUNT shrink another fifty percent.

PAUSE 3 SECONDS

Again snap. GRUNT shrinks another fifty percent.

PAUSE 3 SECONDS

I am now going to stop talking for thirty seconds while you continue snapping your fingers until GRUNT shrinks so much that it disappears. Start snapping now.

PAUSE 30 SECONDS

Very good. When GRUNT shrinks out of sight you may crunch it up in your hand, toss it into a trash can, or throw it down and step on it if you wish as a final destruction of the greedy pest.

It is now an established fact. Whenever GRUNT makes its presence known, all you need to do to get rid of it is to physically open the palm of your hand, put GRUNT into your palm either by seeing or visualizing it there or by picking GRUNT up and placing it in your palm, and then physically pointing your index finger at GRUNT and snapping your fingers repeatedly until GRUNT disappears. GRUNT will shrink fifty percent each time you point and snap. You may also say "Gone" out loud in place of snapping your fingers.

In the future, wherever you are and whatever you are doing you can destroy GRUNT by the method you have just practiced and have had programmed into your mind. You do not need to close your eyes to do this unless you wish to. The moment that you place GRUNT into your hand and begin to point and snap, your mind will automatically alter itself to effectively destroy GRUNT, and this is so. However, you must physically hold out your palm, put GRUNT in it, and physically point and physically snap or else say "Gone" out loud in place of snapping.

You are now equipped with a powerful, effective method of destroying GRUNT. All that remains now is for you to actually do it until you get rid of GRUNT.

Now take a deep breath and relax.

While you are standing in the light in your room, I want you to build an image. An image of yourself as you really want to be. Not as someone else wants you to be, but as you really want yourself to be. See your image standing in front of you in the light. See the quiet look of confidence on the face of your image. Notice how calm and free your image is. I will stop talking now for 60 seconds while you give your image all the qualities and attributes you wish it to have.

PAUSE 60 SECONDS

Now visualize your image doing those things that GRUNT had deprived you of doing in the past. Your image is enjoying doing those things and is happy for this new freedom. In a moment I will stop talking for one minute while you visualize your image doing those things that GRUNT used to deprive you of. If GRUNT should appear, have your image destroy it using the method you have just learned. Do it now. You have one minute.

PAUSE 60 SECONDS

Notice now the look of triumph and confidence on the face of your image. This is the real you. Walk closer to your image now. Walk closer. Now walk into your image. Let it blend into your very body. Your own best self, a living part of you now. Stronger every day.

From now on every day you will be more and more completely the person you really want to be. You will be relaxed and calm. And no matter what is going on around you, you can handle it in a relaxed and sensible manner. And you will feel so good. You will have all the energy you can use every single day. And it will be so easy for you to stay in complete control of every aspect of your life. You will find it very easy to dispel all fears, anxieties, doubts, and troubles. You will find it very quick and easy to destroy and get rid of GRUNT. You are in total control of your life, and this is so.

Now take one final look around your room. You can come back here anytime you wish. You can come here for any purpose you wish . . . to pray . . . to consult with higher mind . . . to set goals . . . to meditate . . . to create . . . to learn . . . to solve problems . . . to make changes to your self-image. What you do in your room has no limit. No limit.

You have just experienced using the altered state of consciousness to go deep within yourself to a private, powerful, creative place that you can use for practical purposes and for spiritual purposes. You have been given this valuable tool to use to enrich your life. Use it every day and design your life the way you want it to be. The choice is yours alone to do or not to do. For you are in control now. And whatever you choose to do, you can do. Whatever you set your own mind to achieve, you can and will achieve it. You will be completely successful and you will enjoy your success. And you will enjoy becoming the person you really want to be more and more every day.

The next time you hear my voice on tape, you will allow yourself to relax ten times more deeply relaxed than you are now. And the suggestions I give you then will go ten times deeper into your mind.

In a few moments when you awaken yourself, you will feel very, very relaxed and you will feel completely refreshed, alive, alert, full of energy, and full of self-confidence.

You will feel simply marvelous. All you have to do to awaken yourself is to mentally count with me from one up to five and at the count of five you will awaken feeling relaxed, refreshed, alert, and in very high spirits. Feeling very good indeed. 1 . . . 2 . . . 3 . . . 4 . . . 5.

SNAP FINGERS

Open eyes, wide awake and feeling fine, feeling better than before, and this is so!

•   •   •

Insomnia
Control

1
1

THIS TAPE will help you to get rid of insomnia and to have a peaceful, relaxing, enjoyable night of sleep.

When your mind is undisciplined, it refuses to relax and refuses to allow your body to relax. As a result, it is very difficult, even impossible at times, to go to sleep.

What must be done is to train your mind to do what you want when you want it to with regard to sleep.

This tape, through self-hypnosis, trains your mind to allow you to sleep when you want to.

Each night when you go to bed, turn the tape on and follow the instructions. If the tape should play all the way through and you have not yet fallen asleep, rewind the tape and continue to listen. Keep at it until you win by falling asleep. The more you use this tape, the less time it will take you to fall asleep. Eventually, you get to the point where you will no longer need to listen to the tape because you will have successfully trained your mind to respond to sleep when you want it to.

The tape may put you to sleep the first time you use it. Or it may take longer. It all depends on you and on how deeply ingrained your insomnia has become. If you persist in using the tape every night, you will conquer your insomnia.

Do not be concerned about turning off the tape player. Just allow yourself to fall asleep. The tape player will shut off automatically at the end of the tape. The instructions from the tape will continue to go deep into your subconscious mind even after you fall asleep. Thus, you continue to benefit from the tape even though your conscious mind is sound asleep.

Insomnia Tape Script

Close your eyes. Take a deep breath, and begin to relax.

I want you to imagine now that you are looking at a clear, blue summer sky. And in the sky, a sky-writing airplane is writing your first name in fluffy, white cloudlike letters. See your name floating fluffy, white, and cloudlike in a clear, blue sky. Now let your name just dissolve away. Let the winds just blow your name away into the blue. Forget about your name. Forget you even have a name. Names are not important. Just go on listening to my voice and allowing yourself to relax more deeply in the direction of peaceful, relaxing sleep.

Focus your attention on your knees now and relax everything below your knees. Relax your calves. Relax your ankles. Relax your feet. And relax your toes. Relax your toes. Everything below your knees is now loose and relaxed. Now relax your thighs as completely as you can. Let your thighs just droop limp and loose and heavy. Relax your hips and relax your waist. Now relax your chest as completely as you can. Allow your breathing to be easier and deeper, more regular and more relaxed. Relax your shoulders now. Let the muscles in your shoulders be heavy and loose. More and more completely relaxed. Relax your neck and throat. Let your head just droop as all the muscles in your neck just relax. Now relax your face as completely as you can. Allow your face to be smooth and loose, relaxed and easy, your jaws all loose and relaxed, your teeth not quite touching. Everything is smooth and loose and easy. Now relax as completely as you can all the little muscles around your eyelids. Feel your eyelids growing heavier and smoother. More and more deeply relaxed.

I want you to imagine now that all your tensions, all your tightness, and all your fears and worries are draining away from the top of your head. Let it drain down through your face, down through your neck, through your shoulders, through your chest, your waist, your hips, your thighs, down through your knees, your calves, your ankles, your feet and out your toes. All your tension, all your tightness, all your worries and fears are draining away now from the very tips of your toes, and you are relaxing more and more.

We are going to do this relaxation exercise again. This time I want you to allow yourself to relax even more fully and completely than you did the first time.

Focus your attention on your knees once again and relax everything below your knees. Relax your calves. Relax your ankles. Relax your feet, and relax your toes. And now relax your thighs even more completely. Allow your thighs to droop limp and heavy. Relax your hips and your waist. Feel the relaxation flowing into your chest now. Relaxing the vital organs within your chest, your heart, your lungs, allowing your breathing to be more intense, more regular, more and more completely relaxed. Now relax your shoulders even more. Feel your shoulders heavy and loose. More and more deeply relaxed. Relax your neck and throat. Relax your face even more. Feel your face all smooth and loose, completely easy and relaxed all over. And now relax even more all the little muscles around your eyelids. Feel your eyelids heavy and smooth, more and more deeply relaxed.

We are going to do this relaxation exercise one more time. This time I want you to allow yourself to relax so completely that your mind and body will drift into blissful sleep. Do not fight sleep. Just listen to my voice while you pull out all the stops and allow yourself to sink into perfect relaxation and into perfect sleep.

Focus your attention again on your knees and relax everything below your knees. Relax your calves, relax your ankles, relax your feet, and relax your toes. Now relax your thighs completely.

Feel the deep and heavy relaxation flowing into your hips now. Feel it going up through your waist, flowing into your chest, to your shoulders, heavy and loose, completely relaxed. And now this heavy relaxed feeling is going into your neck and throat, all over your face. Your face is all smooth and loose, completely easy and relaxed, and the heavy relaxation is flowing into your eyes and eyelids now. Your eyelids are so heavy and so smooth. Ever more deeply relaxed.

Every muscle in your body is relaxed and sleepy. Every cell in your body is deeply relaxed and wants to go to sleep. Your conscious mind is relaxed and sleepy. The soft veil of peaceful sleep now envelops your entire body, and you surrender to sleep. Feel the sleepiness. Feel yourself drifting to sleep. Go to sleep. Sleep. Sleep. Sleep.

I want you to imagine now that you are looking at a blackboard. On the blackboard imagine a circle. Into the circle we are going to place the letters of the alphabet in reverse order, and with each letter after you place it into the circle, you will erase it then from inside the circle and allow yourself to relax more and more deeply in the direction of sleep.

Picture the blackboard now. Picture the circle. Into the circle put the letter Z. Now erase the Z from inside the circle, and go deeper. Put Y into the circle, and erase it and go deeper. X, and erase it and go deeper still. W, and erase it. V, and erase it. U, and erase it. T, and erase it. S, and erase it. R, and erase it. Q, and erase it, P, and erase it. O, and erase it. N, and erase it. M, and erase it. L, and erase it. K, and erase it. J, and erase it. I, and erase it. H, and erase it. G, and erase it. F, and erase it. E, and erase it. D, and erase it. C, and erase it. B, and erase it. A, and erase it. Now erase the circle and forget about the blackboard. Just go on relaxing more and more deeply. Feel yourself sinking into deep sleep. Mind and body drifting deeper and deeper into relaxing sleep, deeper with each breath.

I want you to imagine now that I am placing on each of your knees a heavy bag of sand. Feel the sand pressing down on your knees. Your knees are growing heavier and more relaxed. In the sand is a very powerful numbing ingredient that causes sleep to come to every part of the body. The numbness is flowing down into your knees now. Your knees are growing numb and more numb and sleepy under the sand. And the heavy, numb, sleepy feeling is flowing down into your calves, into your ankles, into your feet and toes. Everything below your knees is numb and more numb and sleepy from the sand. And now the heavy, numb, sleepy feeling is going up into your thighs, flowing into your hips, through your waist, and into your chest. It flows into your shoulders, and they grow numb and heavy and sleepy. It flows down your arms, your upper arms, your forearms, into your hands and fingers. Flowing back now through your forearms, your upper arms, your shoulders, and into your neck. Over your face, your eyes. Flowing up to your eyebrows, your forehead, over the top of your head, down the back of your head, and down the back of your neck.

Your entire body is now heavy, numb, and sleepy. Go to sleep. Sleep. Sleep.

As you breathe in, imagine that you are breathing in a pure, clean, odorless anesthesia. The anesthesia is flowing all throughout your body now. It is a warm, numb, tingling feeling, and the more you breathe in, the more you want to breathe in, and you allow your breathing to become even deeper now, bringing in more and more of this peaceful, relaxing, tranquil feeling. From now on until the end of this session, you will allow yourself to relax more and more completely into deeper and deeper sleep with each breath you take. Go to sleep. Sleep. Sleep.

As you drift into deeper and deeper relaxation and sleep, just listen to my voice and I will direct you into the most peaceful night's sleep you have ever experienced, and this is so.

I am going to take you down through four progressively deeper levels of relaxation and into the deepest, most tranquil sleep of all.

I will label these levels with letters of the alphabet, and when you reach the first level, level A, you will be ten times more deeply relaxed and sleepy than you are even now. And then from level A we will go down to level B, and when you reach level B you will be ten times again more deeply relaxed and sleepy than you were before. And from level B we will go down even further, down to level C. And when you reach level C you will be ten times again more deeply relaxed and sleepy than before. And then from level C we will go all the way down to the deepest level of relaxation and sleep, level D. And when you reach level D, you will be ten times again more deeply relaxed and sleepy than before. You are drifting down now, two times deeper with each breath that you exhale. Two times deeper with each breath. Your hands and fingers are so relaxed and heavy, and they keep growing heavier. Feel the heaviness growing in your hands and fingers. Heavy . . . heavier . . . heavier still until now they are so heavy it is as though your hands and fingers were made of lead. And this deeply relaxed, heavy feeling is flowing up through your forearms now. Feel it going up into your upper arms. Flowing through your shoulders, into your neck, over your face, over your eyes.

Flowing up to your eyebrows, your forehead, over the top of your head. The deep relaxed, heavy feeling is flowing down the back of your head and down the back of your neck. You are now approaching level A.

You are on level A now and still going deeper. Five times deeper now with each breath that you exhale. Five times deeper with each breath. Your mind is so still and peaceful. You're not thinking of anything now. Too relaxed to think. Too comfortable to think. Too sleepy to think. And this heavy relaxation in your mind is flowing into your face and eyes. It is flowing down through your neck and into your chest. Flowing down to your waist, down through your hips, your thighs, your knees, your calves, your ankles, your feet, and your toes. You are now approaching level B.

You are on level B now and still drifting deeper into sleep. Floating smoothly and gently into perfect sleep. Your arms and legs are so relaxed and heavy they feel like logs. Your arms and legs are stiff and numb and heavy . . . simply immovable. Your arms and legs are like planks of wood. You are now approaching level C.

You are on level C now and still drifting down into deeper sleep. Sinking into the bed. Sinking deeper and deeper into perfect relaxation and sleep. And as you go on drifting even deeper, I am going to count backwards from 15 to 1. Each number that I say will take you deeper and deeper still, and when I reach 1 you will be on level D. 15, deeper, 14, deeper still, 13 . . . 12 . . . 11 . . . 10 . . . 9 . . . 8 . . . 7 . . . 6, let it all go now, 5 . . . 4 . . . 3 . . . 2 . . . 1 . . . 1 . . . 1, so deep, so dreamy, so heavy, so misty.

You are now on level D and still drifting down into deeper and deeper sleep. There is no limit now. . . no limit. Go on floating, drifting deeper and deeper into perfect sleep, deeper with each breath.

As you continue to drift deeper and deeper into perfect sleep, I offer these suggestions for your benefit.

These states of deep relaxation are very beneficial to your mental and physical health.

You are now training your conscious mind to relax and to go to sleep whenever you wish to go to sleep. Your conscious mind is responding perfectly by becoming quiet while you drift quickly into healthy, relaxing, restful sleep.

You are learning to relax . . . to release all anxiety and relax and let go. For you are in control of all aspects of your life now. No longer will you allow anxiety, tension, or nervous energy to impede you. Every day you will notice yourself relaxing more. You will notice yourself becoming more calm and more in control than ever before.

You will notice every day that your attitude is becoming more and more philosophical and free of serious concern about life's daily problems.

This tape is training your mind and body so that you will soon be able to go to sleep quickly and easily without even having to listen to the tape, and this is so.

The next time you hear my voice on tape, you will allow yourself to relax ten times more deeply than you are now. And the suggestions I give you then will go ten times deeper into your mind.

Tonight you will experience a relaxing, restful night

of sleep that is just like the deep sleep of a newborn baby. And when you awaken in the morning you will be completely refreshed physically, mentally, and emotionally. You will be full of energy and enthusiasm. Every time you listen to this tape you will relax ten times deeper than before, and you will go to sleep faster and sounder every time, and this is so. Your mind now understands that when you retire for the night that you desire to go to sleep quickly and to sleep deeply. Your mind will cooperate by relaxing you completely right away.

Now relax and drift into peaceful, restful sleep. As you drift deeper into sleep, I will count backwards from 99. Each number that I say will make you become even more relaxed mentally, physically, and emotionally. Each number I say will take you into an even deeper level of sleep.

Just relax and let the numbers take you into a deep sleep.

99, sleep. 98, sleep. 97, sleep. 96, sleep. 95, sleep. (Continue this countdown until reaching 1 or until reaching the end of the tape, whichever comes first.)

● ● ●

Work Success

THIS TAPE will guide you into an altered state of consciousness that will enable you to accept hypnotic suggestions that can ensure your success in your work, your working relationships, and in the general conduct of your performance in your chosen occupation. The suggestions will be programmed in at several levels of your mind for even greater and faster results.

This tape cannot make you do anything you really do not want to do. If you really and truly want to establish a successful, productive, enjoyable, and satisfying career, this tape can help you to work wonders.

You may use this Work Success tape as often as you wish. It probably would be a good idea to use it at least once each day until you are satisfied that your work situation is going where you want it to go; then you can reduce the frequency of listening to the tape if you wish.

You can use this tape all by itself, and it will work quite well. However, you may also want to use it in connection with the Goal Setting and Willpower tape (see next chapter).

If you use this Work Success tape in conjunction with the Goal Setting and Willpower tape, then alternate between the tapes. One day use the Work Success tape. The next day use the Goal Setting and Willpower tape. Then the Work Success tape the following day, and so forth.

For the Goal Setting and Willpower tape, you would write out and program your goal something like this: *I want to perform all my work duties and interpersonal relationships with such integrity and enthusiasm that I will assure my success financially and will achieve the maximum level of self-satisfaction that I desire.* Or use whatever other wording that suits your desires.

Work Success
Tape Script

Close your eyes and take a deep, full breath and exhale completely, all the way to the bottom of your lungs. All out. Do it again now, a deep, full breath and let it all out and relax. One more time, and this time hold your breath when you have filled your lungs with clean, refreshing, relaxing air. Hold it in. Keep your eyes closed. Now let your breath out slowly and feel yourself relaxing all over.

I want you to imagine now that all your tensions, all your tightness, and all your fears and worries are draining away from the top of your head. Let it drain down through your face, down through your neck, through your shoulders, through your chest, your waist, your hips, your thighs, down through your knees, your calves, your ankles, your feet, and out your toes. All your tension, all your tightness, all your worries and fears are draining away now from the very tips of your toes, and you are relaxing more and more.

Focus your attention on your toes now and allow your toes to relax completely. Each toe is loose and heavy. Now let this relaxation flow into your feet, into your ankles, your calves, your knees. Feel it flowing into your thighs, into your hips, into your waist, flowing up into your chest now. Feel your breathing easier and deeper, more regular and more relaxed. Now let the deep relaxed feeling go into your shoulders, down your arms, into your upper arms, your forearms, and into your hands and fingers, and flowing back into your forearms, your upper arms, your shoulders. Flowing into your neck, over your face, your chin, your cheeks, even your ears are relaxed. Feel it flowing into your eyes and eyelids now. Your eyelids are so heavy and smooth. Flowing up into your eyebrows, over your forehead, over the top of your head, down the back of your head, and down the back of your neck.

A new heaviness is starting in your toes now. Twice as heavy as the first time. Imagine a heavy weight on each toe. Feel the heaviness deep and even more relaxed. And this heavy, deep feeling is going into your feet, your ankles, your calves, your knees, going into your thighs, your hips, into your waist. Flowing up into your chest now, relaxing your heart, relaxing your lungs, allowing your breathing to be more intense, more regular, more and more completely relaxed. Now the deep heavy feeling is flowing into your shoulders, and down your arms, your upper arms, your forearms, into your hands and fingers. And now flowing back through your forearms, your upper arms, into your shoulders and into your neck. Flowing over your face, into your eyes, over your eyebrows, over your forehead, over the top of your head, down the back of your head and down the back of your neck. You are now deeply relaxed, loose and limp, and comfortable from the top of your head to the very tip of your toes.

I want you to imagine now that you are looking at a blackboard. On the blackboard imagine a circle. Into the circle we are going to place the letters of the alphabet in reverse order, and with each letter after you place it into the circle, you will erase it then from inside the circle and allow yourself to relax more and more deeply.

Picture the blackboard now. Picture the circle. Into the circle put the letter Z. Now erase the Z from inside the circle, and go deeper. Put Y into the circle, and erase it and go deeper. X, and erase it and go deeper still. W, and erase it. V, and erase it. U, and erase it. T, and erase it. S, and erase it. R, and erase it. Q, and erase it. P, and erase it. O, and erase it. N, and erase it. M, and erase it. L, and erase it. K, and erase it. J, and erase it. I, and erase it. H, and erase it. G, and erase it. F, and erase it. E, and erase it. D, and erase it. C, and erase it. B, and erase it. A, and erase it. Now erase the circle and forget about the blackboard. Just go on relaxing more and more deeply. Feel yourself sink into the chair, mind and body drifting deeper and deeper into relaxation, deeper with each breath.

As you go on floating, drifting smoothly and gently, more and more deeply relaxed with each breath, I offer the following suggestions for your benefit.

You will feel an intense interest in your work, and you will feel a tremendous drive to perform to the best of your ability.

You will handle all situations on the job in a very relaxed, calm, and sensible manner free of tension.

You will provide honest and sincere service for your customers and your employer, knowing that your rewards will follow as a result.

You will notice every day that your attitude is becoming more and more philosophical and free of serious concern about life's daily problems.

Now repeat the following suggestions to yourself with me as I say them.

Every day in every way I am getting better, better, and better.

I am committed to the suggestions I have just received.

I know that success is mine.

Now take a deep breath and relax even more.

I am now going to count from 15 down to 1. Each number I say will take you deeper and when I reach 1 you will be at a much deeper level of mind.

15, feel yourself going deeper. 14, deeper still. 13, deeper and deeper. 12 . . . 11 . . . 10 . . . 9 . . . 8 . . . 7 . . . 6, deeper and deeper . . . 5 . . . 4 . . . 3 . . . 2 . . . 1. You are now at a very deep level of mind and are drifting even deeper with each breath you take.

Take a deep breath and go even deeper.

As you drift into deeper levels of mind, I offer the following suggestions for your benefit.

During your working hours you will feel relaxed and calm. Regardless of what happens, you will handle every situation in a relaxed, calm, and sensible manner free of tension.

You will treat all your co-workers with respect and genuine friendliness, knowing that in return you will receive respect and genuine friendliness.

You are a successful person, and you enjoy your success. Part of your success is your ability to manage your time efficiently. You plan your time and your projects, and you execute your plan promptly without allowing yourself to be distracted.

In your working hours on the job, you will feel a powerful and intense concentration power on your work. You will work very, very fast with a tremendous amount of energy.

Now take a deep breath and go deeper.

Repeat the following suggestions to yourself with me as I say them.

Every day in every way I am getting better, better, and better.

I am committed wholeheartedly to all the suggestions I have just received, and this is so.

I am now going to count from 10 down to 1. Mentally visualize each number as I say it, and when I reach 1 you will be at an even deeper level of mind than you are now.

10 . . . 9 . . . 8 . . . 7 . . . 6 . . . 5 . . . 4 . . . 3 . . . 2 . . . 1. You are now at an even deeper level of mind. As you continue to drift deeper and deeper with each breath I offer the following suggestions for your benefit.

You will make decisions easily on the job, and you will feel great confidence in your decisions.

You are capable and efficient, and your creative mind knows what you can do. Your creative mind will find a way to lead you into the right circumstances and situations to best take advantage of your abilities.

You strongly desire to gain full reward for your worthy efforts, but you do not desire to gain at the expense of someone else. You want total success for yourself with harm to no one.

Now repeat the following suggestions to yourself with me as I say them.

I am totally committed to all the suggestions I receive on this tape.

I am totally committed to treating my employer, my fellow workers, and my customers with dignity, respect, genuine affection, friendliness, and integrity.

I am committed to my total success and to completely enjoying that success. I will allow my creative mind to lead me to that success.

And I desire my success with harm to no one and with benefit for everyone, and this is so.

Now take a deep breath and relax even more.

I want you to imagine yourself now. See yourself as you really want to be, the real you. Alive and energetic, in full control, calm and confident and completely successful in your chosen work. This is you. This is the real you. This is the person you can really come to be. At this moment you are making yourself promise to yourself . . . a commitment to become the real you. This commitment will be with you, stronger every day. From now on, every day you will become more and more completely the person you really want to be. You will be relaxed and calm no matter what is going on around you. And anything that does happen, you can handle it in a relaxed and sensible manner. And you will feel so good. You will have all the energy you need every single day. And it will be very easy for you to achieve the success, self-fulfillment, and happiness you want and deserve. For you are a product of your own thought patterns. Think success, and you are a success. Think beauty and you become a beautiful person. Think strength and you become strong.

Think positively and constructively, and your life becomes a positive and constructive experience. These things are your new image...the new you... stronger and stronger every day.

You are now learning to be in total control of every aspect of your life. You will always be relaxed and calm.

You are your own person, and you are in control.

In a moment, I am going to count backward from 10 to 1.

I want you to count with me silently to yourself. Think each number as I say it, and allow each number to take you deeper. 10 . . . 9 . . . 8 . . . 7 . . . 6 . . . 5 . . . 4 . . . 3 . . . 2 . . . 1. You are now very deeply relaxed. You can give yourself the following suggestions. Say the words to yourself with me as I say them.

I will always be relaxed and calm no matter what is happening. And anything that does happen, I can handle it in a sensible and mature manner.

I think of the present and future only.

I have an optimistic, positive attitude about life and my work.

I love life and my work.

I am becoming more philosophical and free of serious concern about life's daily problems because I know I can handle anything that happens in a beneficial manner.

I have a tremendous and intense concentration power in my work.

I feel positive that everything in my life will work out for me, and I feel good about myself and the direction my life is now going in.

Now take a deep breath and relax even more.

Every time you listen to this tape it makes you feel just wonderful. Each time you listen to this tape you will relax completely, and the suggestions will go deeper and deeper into your mind. By using this tape faithfully every day, you will have perfect control over your life and your work success. You can dissolve away any fear. You can dissolve away any tension. You can dissolve away any feelings of inadequacy. You will keep on performing better and better, and you will keep on feeling good every single day. You are an intelligent and worthwhile person. And every day from now on you will become more completely the person you really want to be. You will be confident, relaxed, poised, charming, optimistic, and firm in your resolution to do what you want for your own happiness.

The next time you hear my voice on tape, you will allow yourself to go even deeper than you are now, and the suggestions I have given you will keep on going deeper and deeper and deeper into your mind.

In a few moments when you awaken yourself, you will feel very, very relaxed, and you will be completely refreshed, alive, alert, full of energy, full of confidence. You will feel simply marvelous. All you have to do to awaken is to count with me from one up to five and at the count of five, open your eyes, feeling relaxed, refreshed, alert, in very high spirits. Feeling very good indeed. 1 . . . 2 . . . 3 . . . 4 . . . 5.

● ● ●

Goal Setting and Willpower

THIS TAPE is one you will want to use frequently—either by itself or in conjunction with one of the other tapes. If you use it in conjunction with another tape, program the specific goal you wanted on this tape and then alternate playing this tape with the other one. For example, if you used this Goal Setting tape in conjunction with the Diet Control tape, you would use the Diet Control tape one day, and use this Goal Setting tape the next day, and so forth. For diet, you would create an appropriate goal on this tape such as: *I want to have the willpower to stay strictly on the diet I have set for myself, and I want to lose my excess weight so that I will no longer be overweight.* Or for smoking cessation, you might put in a goal such as: *I want to totally stop using tobacco in all of its forms and become a non-smoker.* You can use this tape in conjunction with virtually any other tape to strengthen your program.

This Goal Setting and Willpower tape is also very effective all by itself for setting and realizing all of your goals.

The tape also strengthens your willpower to achieve whatever it is you want. Use this tape frequently for all goals, large and small. Some examples: to smile more frequently; to improve your work performance; to become more friendly; to get rid of shyness; to get a new or better job; to earn more money; to read or study more effectively. There is no end to the possibilities.

Here is how to use this tape. First write a single goal on a piece of paper and have it near you for use during the hypnosis session. You may have two goals on the paper if they are closely related to each other.

If you have many goals, I strongly recommend that you handle them separately in individual hypnosis sessions that are spaced at least one hour apart. There is no limit as to how many goals you can have and program for, but just handle them separately. If you do, you will find you get much more effective results. When you become really experienced at this, then you can start grouping goals together in one session. But for beginners, do one—two at the most—in a single session.

Use this tape as often as you wish. You should use it at least once a week for each goal until you attain that goal.

At one point in this self-hypnosis procedure you will be directed to open your eyes and read the goal you have written on the paper. There will be a two-minute pause in the talking while you do this. If you should finish reading it before the talking resumes, just reread the goal. Keep reading it until the tape directs you to close your eyes.

If for some reason you are not able to write your goals or to read them, then when the tape directs you to open your eyes and read, just keep your eyes closed and mentally repeat your goals over and over until the tape resumes talking.

Goal Setting and Willpower
Tape Script

Close your eyes and take a deep, full breath and exhale completely, all the way to the bottom of your lungs. All out. Do it again now. Just relax and let it all out. One more time, and this time hold your breath when you have filled your lungs with clean, refreshing, relaxing air. Hold it in. Keep your eyes closed. Now let your breath out slowly and feel yourself relaxing all over.

I want you to imagine now that all your tensions, all your tightness, and all your fears and worries are draining away from the top of your head. Let it drain down through your face, down through your neck, through your shoulders, through your chest, your waist, your hips, your thighs, down through your knees, your calves, your ankles, your feet, and out your toes. All your tension, all your tightness, all your worries and fears are draining away now from the very tips of your toes, and you are relaxing more and more.

Focus your attention on your toes now and allow your toes to relax completely. Each toe is loose and heavy. Now let this relaxation flow into your feet, into your ankles, your calves, your knees. Feel it flowing into your thighs, into your hips, into your waist, flowing up into your chest now. Feel your breathing easier and deeper, more regular and more relaxed. Now let the deep relaxed feeling go into your shoulders, down your arms, into your upper arms, your forearms, and into your hands and fingers, and flowing back into your forearms, your upper arms, your shoulders. Flowing into your neck, over your face, your chin, your cheeks, even your ears are relaxed. Feel it flowing into your eyes and eyelids now. Your eyelids are so heavy and smooth. Flowing up into your eyebrows, over your forehead, over the top of your head, down the back of your head, and down the back of your neck.

A new heaviness is starting in your toes now. Twice as heavy as the first time. Imagine a heavy weight on each toe. Feel the heaviness deep and even more relaxed. And this heavy, deep feeling is going into your feet, your ankles, your calves, your knees, going into your thighs, your hips, into your waist. Flowing up into your chest now, relaxing your heart, relaxing your lungs, allowing your breathing to be more intense, more regular, more and more completely relaxed. Now the deep heavy feeling is flowing into your shoulders, and down your arms, your upper arms, your forearms, into your hands and fingers. And now flowing back through your forearms, your upper arms, into your shoulders and into your neck. Flowing over your face, into your eyes, over your eyebrows, over your forehead, over the top of your head, down the back of your head and down the back of your neck.

And a new heaviness is starting now at the top of your head. Twice as heavy as before. Twice as heavy. Imagine a heavy weight on the very top of your head, soft and relaxed and heavy. Feel the heavy relaxation flowing down into your face and eyes now, down through your neck, your shoulders, flowing down through your chest, your waist, your hips, your thighs, your knees, into your calves, your ankles, your feet and toes. Deeply relaxed, loose and limp, and comfortable from the top of your head to the very tip of your toes.

I want you to imagine now that you are looking at a blackboard. On the blackboard imagine a circle. Into the circle we are going to place the letters of the alphabet in reverse order, and with each letter after you place it into the circle, you will erase it then from inside the circle and allow yourself to relax more and more deeply.

Picture the blackboard now. Picture the circle. Into the circle put the letter Z. Now erase the Z from inside the circle, and go deeper. Put Y into the circle, and erase it and go deeper. X, and erase it and go deeper still. W, and erase it. V, and erase it. U, and erase it. T, and erase it. S, and erase it. R, and erase it. Q, and erase it. P, and erase it. O, and erase it. N, and erase it. M, and erase it. L, and erase it. K, and erase it. J, and erase it. I, and erase it. H, and erase it. G, and erase it. F, and erase it. E, and erase it. D, and erase it. C, and erase it. B, and erase it. A, and erase it. Now erase the circle and forget about the blackboard. Just go on relaxing more and more deeply. Feel yourself sink into the chair, mind and body drifting deeper and deeper into relaxation, deeper with each breath.

As you breathe in, imagine that you are breathing in a pure, clean, odorless anesthesia. The anesthesia is flowing all throughout your body now. It is a warm, numb, tingling feeling, and the more you breathe in, the more you want to breathe in, and you allow your breathing to become even deeper now, bringing in more and more of this peaceful, relaxing, tranquil feeling. From now on until the end of this session, you will allow yourself to relax more and more completely with each breath you take.

I want you to imagine now that you are looking at a clear, blue summer sky. And in the sky, a sky-writing airplane is writing your first name in fluffy, white cloudlike letters. See your name floating fluffy, white, and cloudlike in a clear, blue sky. Now let your name just dissolve away. Let the winds just blow your name away into the blue. Forget about your name. Forget you even have a name. Names are not important. Just go on listening to my voice and allowing yourself to relax more deeply.

I want you to imagine now that you are standing on the top step of a heavy wooden staircase. Feel the carpet under your feet. The carpet can be any kind and color you wish...create it. Now extend your hand out and touch the railing. Feel the smooth polished wood of the railing under your hand. You are standing just ten steps up from the floor below. The stairs are curving very smoothly down to the floor below. In a moment we will walk down the stairs. With each step down you will allow yourself to relax even more deeply. By the time you reach the floor below you will be deeper than you have ever gone before. Take a step down now, down to the ninth step smoothly and easily. Feel yourself going deeper. Now down to eight, deeper still. Now down to seven . . . six . . . five . . . four . . . three . . . two . . . one. Now you are standing on the floor below. There is a door in front of you. Reach out and open the door. And from the room beyond the door a flood of light comes streaming out through the open doorway. Walk into the room, into the light through the open door. You are inside the room now, look around you. This is your room, and it can be anything you want it to be. Any size, any shape, any colors. You can have anything in this room that you want. You can add things, remove things, rearrange things. You can have any kind of furniture, fixtures, paintings, windows, carpets, or whatever you want because this is your place...your very own private inner place and you are free here. Free to create, free to be who you are. Free to do whatever you will, and the light that shines in this room is your light. Feel the light all around you, shining on the beautiful things in your room. Shining on you; feel the energy in the light. Let the light flow all through your body now. Going in through every pore in your skin. Filling you completely. Pushing away all doubt. Pushing out all fear and tension. You are filled with the light. You are clear and radiant, glowing with the shining light in your room.

While you are standing in the light in your room, I want you to program the personal goal you have in mind or have written on a paper before starting this session.

In a few moments I will ask you to open your eyes and to read the goal you have written on your paper. When you open your eyes you will not awaken. You will not awaken. I will then stop talking for two minutes while you read and concentrate on your goal. Now open your eyes and read your goal.

PAUSE 120 SECONDS

Now close your eyes. Take a deep breath and go deeper. Your goal is going deeper and deeper into your mind with each breath you take.

I want you to imagine now . . . to visualize your goal. See yourself with your goal already achieved. Let your imagination picture the success of your goal. I will stop talking now for one minute while you do this.

PAUSE 60 SECONDS

Now take a deep breath and go deeper.

Your goal is now reality at a mental and spiritual level. It is now only a matter of time, persistence, patience, practice, and perseverance until your goal becomes reality in the physical world, and this is so.

I am now going to count from ten down to one. Visualize and mentally say the numbers with me as I say them. Allow each number to take you deeper.

10, feel going deeper, 9 deeper still, 8 . . . 7 . . . 6 . . . deeper and deeper . . . 5 . . . 4 . . . 3 . . . 2 . . . 1. You are now at a very deep level of mind. You can now give yourself the following suggestions. Repeat them to yourself as I say them.

Every day my willpower becomes stronger and stronger.

I am determined to achieve my goals and to live my life the way I want.

I will not allow other people or situations to run my life. I am in control of my life, and that is the way I want it to be.

I will not give in to temptations that I know are contrary to what I want. I will remain firm in all my resolutions. I will not give in to anything I really do not want or need.

I am a good, worthwhile, and strong-willed person and I like who I am. And every day I become better and stronger in every way.

Now take a deep breath and relax even more.

Each time you listen to this tape you will become ten times more deeply relaxed than before, and the suggestions you receive on this tape will be stronger and go deeper into your mind all the time. For you are in control now. Whatever you choose to do, you can do. Whatever you set your mind to achieve, you can and will achieve. You will be completely successful, and you will enjoy your success. And you will enjoy having more and more willpower every day, and you will enjoy experiencing the fulfillment of your goals.

Now take a deep breath and relax.

In a few moments when you awaken yourself, you will feel very, very relaxed, and you will be completely refreshed, alive, alert, full of energy, full of confidence. You will feel simply marvelous. All you have to do to awaken is to count with me from one up to five and at the count of five, open your eyes, feeling relaxed, refreshed, alert, in very high spirits. Feeling very good indeed. 1 . . . 2 . . . 3 . . . 4 . . . 5.

•   •   •

Creative Visualization

14

THIS IS a different kind of tape. This tape trains your mind to visualize more effectively. Visualization is the key to obtaining faster and more profound results from self-hypnosis and psychic practice. Though I haven't mentioned it previously in this book, self-hypnosis is a highly effective way of launching into the development of your innate psychic ability. In fact, some of the procedures actually do take you into the psychic realm and enable you to perform some basic psychic functions such as telepathy. Some of the "Love Tapes" and the "World Peace" tapes are examples. What your mind can picture, it can achieve much more easily.

This tape is very beneficial, and it is fun. You will learn to see in color, to visualize shapes, to create scenes, to create specific objects, and to change things.

Many people are not used to visualizing. It is a learned skill. Therefore, do not become discouraged if you are not able to visualize perfectly when you first start out. If your mental pictures just don't materialize or are hazy, use your imagination; pretend that the pictures and colors and shapes are there and continue using the tape. Eventually you will start to develop colors, shapes, and pictures like you want. For some people, visualization comes instantly. For others it takes quite a long time and lots of persistence. Remember you are training your mind, and your mind can sometimes act like a reluctant child. With a reluctant child you must repeat, repeat, and repeat until you get the desired response. It is the same way with your mind.

You may listen to this tape as often as you wish. It is good practice.

Creative Visualization Tape Script

Stretch your right arm and left leg and relax. Now stretch your left arm and right leg and relax. Now stretch both arms and both legs . . . all over . . . and relax. Flop your arms and legs into a lazy, comfortable position and close your eyes.

To take a balloon breath, you breathe in through your nose and see a balloon coming toward you. To blow out a balloon breath, you blow out through your mouth and blow the balloon away. And when you get to your favorite place, remember to be very still and quiet.

Now see before you a red balloon. Take a balloon breath through your nose; see the red balloon come toward you. Now blow the red balloon away by blowing out through your mouth.

See before you an orange balloon. Take a balloon breath through your nose; see the orange balloon come toward you. Now blow the orange balloon away by blowing out through your mouth.

See a yellow balloon. Take a balloon breath and see the yellow balloon come toward you. Now blow the yellow balloon away.

See a green balloon. Take a balloon breath and see the green balloon come toward you. Now blow the green balloon away.

See a blue balloon. Take a balloon breath and see the blue balloon come toward you. Now blow the blue balloon away.

Now breathe in and see the number 10. Hold the breath and see 9. Breathe out and see 8. Breathe in and see 7. Hold the breath and see 6. Breathe out and see 5. Breathe in and see 4. Hold the breath and see 3. Breathe out and see 2.

Now see the number 1 tied to a purple balloon. Grab hold of the 1 and blow yourself away to your favorite place. Your favorite place can be anywhere you want. It can have anything you want in it, because it is your place, your very own place. I will stop talking for 30 seconds while you blow yourself to your favorite place. Create and see your favorite place.

PAUSE 30 SECONDS

Take a balloon breath and you will feel great. You will relax more in your favorite place. When you want to remember something, take a balloon breath and see the answer behind your eyes. To be in charge of yourself, take a balloon breath. You will do whatever you believe you can do. Give yourself a hug with your elbow for being a special person. Now send a mental hug to someone special.

PAUSE 3 SECONDS

You are now learning how to visualize in your mind so that you can be more effective in using your mind for whatever worthwhile purpose you desire.

Now it is time to leave your favorite place and go to a special chair where you will practice more visualization. To leave now, take a balloon breath through your nose. See a white balloon with your favorite stripes on it. Hold onto the striped balloon and blow yourself back. The striped balloon is taking you to a large, comfortable chair. The balloon is lowering you into the chair. Now let go of the striped balloon and watch it float up and away.

Now examine the chair you are sitting in. It is a soft, blue velvet chair. See it. On the arms of the chair are special button controls. By pushing these buttons you can cause certain things to happen as you will see in a few moments.

I want you to press the button on the left arm of your chair now. A blackboard lowers from above you to just in front of you where you can reach it. The blackboard has a chalk tray containing an eraser and several pieces of white chalk. Take a moment to study the details of the blackboard.

PAUSE 2 SECONDS

Now pick up a piece of the chalk and draw a triangle on the blackboard. Now put the number 3 inside the triangle. Study the triangle with the number 3 inside it.

PAUSE 2 SECONDS

Pick up the eraser and erase the triangle and the number. Study the blank blackboard.

PAUSE 2 SECONDS

Now draw a square on the blackboard. Write the number 4 inside the square. Study the square with the number 4 in it for a moment and then erase it from the blackboard until it is all gone.

PAUSE 2 SECONDS

Now draw a circle on the blackboard. Write your first name inside the circle. Study the circle with your name in it.

PAUSE 2 SECONDS

Now erase it all away.

Press the button again, and watch the blackboard raise up out of sight.

You are learning to create shapes at will and to remove them at will.

In a moment I am going to ask you to press the button on the right-hand arm of your chair. When you press it, seven colored balls will enter your head one at a time from your right and pass through your head just behind your eyes and then exit through the left side of your head.

Press the button on the right arm of your chair now and watch the colored balls. A red ball enters the right side of your head. Watch it float through your head just behind your eyes and exit the left side of your head.

PAUSE 2 SECONDS

Now an orange ball enters. Watch it float through your head and leave.

PAUSE 2 SECONDS

Now a yellow ball enters; watch it.

PAUSE 1 SECOND

Now a green ball enters and floats through; watch it.

PAUSE 1 SECOND

Now a light blue ball floats through.

PAUSE 1 SECOND

Now a dark blue ball.

PAUSE 1 SECOND

And now a purple ball floats through and leaves.

Now press the same button again and the balls will float rapidly back through your head in reverse order from left to right. Press the button.

Here comes the purple ball. Followed by the dark blue ball. Followed by the light blue ball. Followed by the green ball. Followed by the yellow ball. Followed by the orange ball. Followed by the red ball.

Now all the colored balls are gone. Your mind is learning to see colors vividly and to see the colors change rapidly.

I want you to imagine now that you have a slide projector in the very back of your head. You can operate this projector by pressing either button on your chair. When you press a button, the projector in your head will project a picture on a screen at the front of your head. Your screen may be on the inside of your forehead or it may be outside your head about one foot in front of your closed eyes.

In a moment when I ask you, you will project a picture onto your screen of the front of your house or apartment where you live. You have seen the front of your house many times. You know exactly what it looks like. Now, press a button and project the picture of the front of your house or apartment. Study it in detail. Take note of all the colors. The architecture. Everything. You may bring the picture into clear focus by adjusting the focus control on your projector.

PAUSE 5 SECONDS

Now press the button again and project a picture of your favorite animal. Study it. Note the shape. The color. All detail. Adjust your focus control if necessary.

PAUSE 5 SECONDS

Now press the button again and project the picture of someone you love very much. You know this face well. Study it in every detail. Take your time. Adjust your focus control if you need to.

PAUSE 5 SECONDS

Now press the button again to turn off your projector for a while.

You have just experienced learning how to project an image in your mind.

I want you to imagine now that there is a rectangular kitchen table sitting in front of you. Use your imagination to create it.

Now put a blue tablecloth on the table.

Now put a whole cantaloupe on the tablecloth. Notice how the beige outer rind contrasts against the blue tablecloth. Put a large butcher knife on the table. Pick up the knife and cut the cantaloupe in half. Examine the juicy, orange interior flesh of the melon.

Notice the cluster of seeds that are in the center of the cut cantaloupe. Notice the contrast of the orange fruit against the blue tablecloth.

Now remove the cantaloupe and the tablecloth. Put a red tablecloth on the table now. Place a head of green lettuce on the tablecloth. Notice the contrast of the green lettuce against the red tablecloth. Now remove the lettuce and the tablecloth.

Now put a black and white checkered tablecloth on the table. Put a vase of red and yellow roses in the center of the table. Study the scene. Notice the detail. How many red roses are there? How many yellow roses are there? What color is the vase? What is the vase made of?

You are now learning to visualize more complex pictures and to analyze the detail in them.

Now let the table and its contents just disappear.

I want you to imagine now that you are at the race track. See yourself sitting in the bleachers. You have a good seat. Notice the people all around you. In front of you. Behind you. On both sides of you.

Now look down below at the race track. There are four race horses on the track. They are prancing around, showing off before the start of the race. A solid black horse has a red saddle blanket on it with a yellow number 1 on the blanket. Study this horse. Pick up your binoculars from your lap and focus on this horse to get a clearer view. Study each detail.

PAUSE 5 SECONDS

Now turn your attention to the big brown horse that has the orange saddle blanket with a black number 2 on it. Study this horse through your binoculars for a clear picture. Analyze each detail.

PAUSE 5 SECONDS

Now train your binoculars on the gray horse wearing the blue blanket with a gold number 3 on it. Study this horse carefully for all the details.

PAUSE 5 SECONDS

Now look at the reddish horse wearing the white blanket with a green number 4 on it. Study this horse carefully.

PAUSE 5 SECONDS

Now put your binoculars back onto your lap and look at all four horses at this distance. Watch them prance around.

They are now lining up side by side to start the race. Pick out the one you think will win.

The signal to start the race has sounded, and the horses leap forward on a hard run. Watch them run. Who is in the lead?

They are coming around the far turn now. Which is first at this point? Which is second? Which is third? Which horse is in fourth place?

They are charging down the final stretch now. They are clustered in a tight group, each one trying to surge into the lead. Then one horse does surge ahead and crosses the finish line first. Which horse won the race? Was it your horse?

Now let the horses and the racetrack fade from view.

You are now learning to create scenes with action, color, detail, and complexity.

Now your final visualization training exercise will be an even more detailed and complex scene.

Take a deep breath and relax even more.

Find yourself lying on a soft, green meadow of grass with the bright sun overhead. Notice the flowers around your head. A gentle breeze ripples across your body. Notice the grass and flowers spring up to about a foot above your head. See how the breeze gently blows the blades of grass back and forth. Smell the fragrance of the flowers.

Now stand up and look to the north. See the majestic mountain at the end of this meadow. Let's take a trip up that mountain. There is a stream to the right of you. Bend down and notice the cool water. Take a drink of this absolutely pure, clean, cool, refreshing water. Listen to the rush of the small rapids on this bubbly brook.

Since the stream seems to come from the mountain, let's follow it. Now we come upon a pond that is at the head of this stream. Notice how warm the water is here. Since at this level of mind we are all expert swimmers, let's go for a swim. Feel the warm sun. Feel the warm water surrounding your body as you quietly move through the water.

It is now time for us to continue up the mountain. As we climb, listen to the birds chirping. Smell the pine trees. Look at the rocks on the bank to our left. Once in a while, we can see the valley and our meadow down below on the right between the trees. We are halfway up the mountain now. Let's stop to rest on the rock to our right. Our meadow is in full view from here. It is now time to continue up to the top of the mountain. Listen to the squirrels chatter in the trees above.

The breeze is blowing the smell of the small cedar trees to us as we near the top. We are on the top now. We can see a deep canyon on the other side. There is a sign on the top of our mountain. It says, "Yell the questions you most want answered into the canyon below, and see the answer written in the sky above." So yell your question now . . . and see the answer in the sky above. Now ask another question. See the answer in the sky above.

Now it is time for us to return to our meadow. See the sun starting to set on the hills to the left. If we hurry, we can be off our mountain before it gets dark. Halfway down the mountain now, and we stop to rest on our rock again. We can watch the beginning of the sunset. Start on down the mountain again. Hear the chirping of the small night animals. Passing our pond, we see the reflection of the sunset in its mirror surface. Our small stream is cool and refreshing as we pass along its side. Now we are back to our meadow. Lie down again in the tall grass. Smell again the flowers' fragrance. Notice the grass and flowers return to their original height as our meadow and mountain now gently fade from view.

Now take a deep breath and relax.

Each time you listen to this tape, your ability to visualize will become stronger, deeper, and more vivid than ever before. Each time you listen to this tape, your visualizations will come faster than ever before, and your imagery will be more detailed and complete, and this is so. You will see everything in color, and you will have perfect control over creating any mental picture that you want. You are training your mind to visualize perfectly, and every time you listen to this tape you get better and better at it.

In a few moments when you awaken yourself, you will feel very, very relaxed, and you will be completely refreshed, alive, alert, full of energy, full of confidence. You will feel simply marvelous. All you have to do to awaken is to mentally count with me from one up to five and at the count of five, open your eyes, feeling relaxed, refreshed, alert, in very high spirits. Feeling very good indeed. 1 . . . 2 . . . 3 . . . 4 . . . 5.

•   •   •

Putting Self in Balance

15

THIS TAPE will guide you into an altered state of consciousness that is deeply relaxing and peaceful. While in that altered state you will be guided through a beautiful procedure that will put you into balance.

What is meant by putting self into balance?

Quite simply, it means to get rid of all the garbage that has been cluttering up your mind and spirit so you will have a clean slate, so to speak. You get rid of negativism such as guilt, hate, anger, and so forth, and replace it with love, faith, forgiveness, and other such positive qualities.

You close the door to the negative aspects of your past, and you open the door to a bright, new, promising future. How a person regards their past can be healthy and beneficial or it can be unhealthy and detrimental. The people who draw on the lessons and experience of the past to better enable them to deal with the present are using the past in a healthy, beneficial way. The people who dwell on the past and continue to live there in their minds to the detriment of enjoying their present are using the past in an unhealthy way. Part of the balancing process is to close the door to the past in order to live in the present in such a way as to ensure a bright future. Going through this procedure does not prevent you from going into your past during hypnotic regression. This balancing procedure merely puts the past into proper perspective for you.

Why is it important to be in balance?

Because life is full of potential enrichment that is yours for the taking. But it is not possible to take it if you are out of balance and impregnated with a predominance of negativism. In the non-physical world, like attracts like. This means that if you are dominated by negativism you will attract negative events into your life. Conversely, if you are dominated by positive energies you will attract positive events into your life.

Did you ever wonder why some people seem to be plagued by misery, bad luck, sickness, and so forth, while others seem to lead a charmed life full of rewards? If you could look into the minds of each you would see two entirely different kinds of thought patterns. The first would likely be filled with fears, hatred, vindictiveness, jealousy, feelings of inferiority, guilt, and so forth. The second would have little or none of those things. Instead there would be feelings of self-worthiness, forgiveness, love, confidence, and so forth. The choice as to which kind of person you want to be is entirely yours. Simply put: you can choose to be a loser or choose to be a winner.

This tape takes you on your first significant step toward becoming a winner in life.

You may use this tape as often as you wish. It makes you feel great, and it keeps you in balance.

Personal Balance
Tape Script

Close your eyes and take a deep, full breath and then exhale all the way to the bottom of your lungs. All out. Now once again take a deep breath and then let it all out. One more time a deep breath and hold it when you get it in. Hold it in. Keep your eyes closed. Now exhale completely and allow yourself to begin to relax more and more.

I want you to imagine now that all your tensions, all your tightness, and all your fears and worries are draining away from the top of your head. Let it drain down through your face, down through your neck, through your shoulders, through your chest, your waist, your hips, your thighs, down through your knees, your calves, your ankles, your feet, and out your toes. All your tension, all your tightness, all your worries and fears are draining away now from the very tips of your toes, and you are relaxing more and more.

Focus your attention on your toes now and allow your toes to relax completely. Each toe is loose and heavy. Now let this relaxation flow into your feet, into your ankles, your calves, your knees. Feel it flowing into your thighs, into your hips, into your waist, flowing up into your chest now. Feel your breathing easier and deeper, more regular and more relaxed.

Now let the deep relaxed feeling go into your shoulders, down your arms, into your upper arms, your forearms, and into your hands and fingers, and flowing back into your forearms, your upper arms, your shoulders.

Flowing into your neck, over your face, your chin, your cheeks, even your ears are relaxed. Feel it flowing into your eyes and eyelids now. Your eyelids are so heavy and smooth. Flowing up into your eyebrows, over your forehead, over the top of your head, down the back of your head, and down the back of your neck.

A new heaviness is starting now at the top of your head. Twice as heavy as before. Twice as heavy. Imagine a heavy weight on the very top of your head, soft and relaxed and heavy. Feel the heavy relaxation flowing down into your face and eyes now, down through your neck, your shoulders, flowing down through your chest, your waist, your hips, your thighs, your knees, into your calves, your ankles, your feet and toes. Deeply relaxed, loose and limp, and comfortable from the top of your head to the very tip of your toes.

I want you to imagine now that you have a valve on the very top of your head. A large unbreakable balloon is attached to the valve. The balloon is not inflated. In a few moments I am going to ask you to open the valve so all the negative garbage in your mind, body, and spirit can escape into the balloon and fill it up. A strong pressure starting at the soles of your feet will force all the negative garbage up into the balloon. Now I want you to reach up and open the valve on top of your head completely. Open it all the way.

Very good. Now imagine a powerful pressure in the soles of your feet. Allow this powerful pressure to begin to move upwards through your feet and ankles forcing ahead of it all the negative garbage. The garbage is forced upward and into the balloon. See the balloon begin to fill up. The pressure moves firmly up into your calves, your knees, your thighs and hips. Garbage pours rapidly upward into the balloon, and the balloon gets fuller and fuller. The pressure continues upward into your waist and chest, pushing ahead of it all the negative energies. The balloon gets bigger. The pressure continues pressing upward through your shoulders, neck, your face and right to the top of your head, forcing every bit of negative garbage and energy out of your entire mind, body, and spirit and into the balloon.

See the balloon full of the black, nasty, negative garbage that used to be in you.

Now reach up and close the valve so the negative mess in the balloon cannot ever come back down into you. Now reach up and tie the neck of the balloon tightly with an unbreakable cord. Tie it tightly shut. Now pull the balloon off the valve so the balloon is free to float upwards forever into space where it can never return to earth. Watch the balloon float higher and higher until it is out of sight. Because the balloon is unbreakable, the negative load it contains can never be released to ever harm anyone. Feel how relieved and peaceful you are now that you are rid of all that unpleasant, negative load. You are free of it from now on, and you are happy about that.

I want you to imagine now that you are looking at a blackboard. On the blackboard imagine a circle. Into the circle we are going to place the letters of the alphabet in reverse order, and with each letter after you place it into the circle, you will erase it then from inside the circle and allow yourself to relax more and more deeply.

Picture the blackboard now. Picture the circle. Into the circle, put the letter Z. Now erase Z from inside the circle, and go deeper. Put Y into the circle, and erase it and go deeper. X, and erase it and go deeper still. W, and erase it. V, and erase it. U, and erase it. T, and erase it. S, and erase it. R, and erase it. Q, and erase it. P, and erase it. O, and erase it. N, and erase it. M, and erase it. L, and erase it. K, and erase it. J, and erase it. I, and erase it. H, and erase it. G, and erase it. F, and erase it. E, and erase it. D, and erase it. C, and erase it. B, and erase it. A, and erase it. Now erase the circle and forget about the blackboard. Just go on relaxing more and more deeply. Feel yourself sink into the chair, mind and body drifting deeper and deeper into relaxation, deeper with each breath.

As you breathe in, imagine that you are breathing in a pure, clean, odorless anesthesia. The anesthesia is flowing all throughout your body now. It is a warm, numb, tingling feeling, and the more you breathe in, the more you want to breathe in, and you allow your breathing to become even deeper now, bringing in more and more of this peaceful, relaxing, tranquil feeling. From now until the end of this session, you will allow yourself to relax more and more completely with each breath you take.

I want you to imagine now that you are looking at a clear, blue summer sky. And in the sky, a sky-writing airplane is writing your first name in fluffy, white cloudlike letters. See your name floating fluffy, white, and cloudlike in a clear, blue sky. Now let your name just dissolve away. Let the winds just blow your name away into the blue. Forget about your name. Forget you even have a name. Names are not important. Just go on listening to my voice and allowing yourself to relax more deeply.

Picture yourself sitting on a large rock outcropping by the ocean with the sea about twenty feet below . . . notice the roar as the ocean rushes in and hits the rocks below you . . . smell the salt air as the wind gushes against your face . . . notice the contrast between your rocks and the beach.

Notice the sea gulls in the sky above . . . watch them dive for their dinner in the sea below . . . listen to their chatter as they return to the sky . . . notice the other birds around you . . . they show their appreciation for life in their smooth gliding and happy song.

Look behind you and you see a trail to your beach . . . walk down that trail to your beach below . . . the smooth path seems to indicate how many people have climbed down from your rock before you . . . these ageless rocks seem to reassure you of the beauty of life, and how being in harmony with nature seems to give you grace . . . the stones and rocks seem to make a slight set of natural stairs about halfway down . . . now back to the sloping trail . . . the sand is warming up and is so inviting . . . the warm sun feels so good . . . take off your shoes and stockings. Leave them here on the sand where you can get them when you return. Now finish your walk to the beach barefooted . . . feel the warm sand squish up between your toes . . . feel the breeze warm you as you reach the beach . . . you are on wet sand now . . . feel its cool firmness under your feet . . . notice how differently this sand feels compared to the warm, dry sand you were on moments ago . . . look at the majestic expanse of ocean in front of you. It stretches as far as you can see. A gentle wave comes ashore and rushes past your feet. Feel how it tugs at you as it recedes back to the ocean. This ocean is the infinite sea of never-ending life and consciousness. Wade out into the water a short distance to where the water comes to your knees. This sea, of which you are a part, contains all the power you will ever need. Feel the power coming from the ocean floor up through your feet and legs, bringing with it love and zest for life. Bringing with it courage and faith. Stand there and allow this priceless gift from the sea to fill your entire body. Flowing up through your legs. Into the trunk of your body. Flowing into your neck and head. You are filled from the sea of consciousness and life. You feel vibrant with love for life and for all. A powerful peace settles over you. Courage has filled every facet of your being. You know you can handle anything in a sensible and beneficial manner. You fear nothing at all. You have no fear, and this is so. Tremendous faith races through you. There is no room for doubt, and you have no doubts. You have received faith, courage, power, and zest for life from this infinite source of goodness. Now walk back to the beach to the point where an occasional wave washes past your ankles.

Bend down and write in the wet sand with your finger this message: "I love . . . " Now under your "I love" message write the names of all those special people you wish to send love. Be sure to include your own name. I will stop talking while you write the names.

PAUSE 60 SECONDS

If you have not yet written your own name, do so quickly now. Now a wave from the sea of consciousness washes up over your message and past your ankles. The wave recedes, washing the beach clean. Your love message has been carried into the sea of universal consciousness where it has become reality.

Bend down and write in the wet sand once more. This time write "I forgive" followed by your own name first, and then the names of all whom you believe have wronged you in some way. I will give you time now to do this.

PAUSE 60 SECONDS

Now at the end of your list write these words: "AND ALL OTHERS."

PAUSE 3 SECONDS

Now another wave from the sea of infinite consciousness washes over your message and past your ankles. When the wave retreats to the sea it takes with it your message of forgiveness which has now become reality. You have now purged yourself of guilt, blame, and animosity. You have filled your life with love, courage, faith, and zest. You are in balance and in harmony with all. You are now ready to serve with integrity and success.

Now stand up and face the sea of life once again. Turn your head to the right and look up the beach . . . that is the direction of the past. There is an open door a short distance from you in that direction. Now turn your head around to your left and look up the beach in that direction . . . that is the direction of the future. There is a closed door a short distance from you in that direction.

Now look back toward the sea of life and consciousness. The breeze from the ocean brings you the awareness of what you must do now . . . you must close the door to the past and open the door to the future. So turn to your right now and walk to the open door of the past. The door has a big sign on it that reads THE PAST. There is a key hanging on a nail on the doorjamb. Take the key into your hand. Take one brief look through the open doorway . . . you see all the mistakes, grief, and wasted energies that once were a part of your life. Now pull the door firmly shut and lock it with the key. Now turn and throw the key far out into the sea, never to be recovered. You have closed and locked the door to all negative aspects of your past. Never again will you need to look through that door. What occurred behind that door is over forever. It is not you now in this present moment.

If you ever decide to go through the door to your past in order to regress into past life experiences you will be able to do so with no problem. What you have just done now in locking the door to the past is to prevent all negative aspects of the past from invading your present and influencing your present life in a negative way.

Now turn around and walk up the beach to the closed door of the future . . . as you approach the door you notice a sign on the door that says THE FUTURE. There is a golden key hanging from the doorjamb. Take the key in your hand and unlock the door. Open the door wide and look through. You see yourself as you really want to be and as you are now becoming. You see brightness and light. You see success and harmony. Take a few moments to get a brief glimpse of your future.

PAUSE 10 SECONDS

You have now opened the door to your future . . . to new hope . . . to new achievement and understanding . . . to a new you. Feel good about yourself.

Now walk back toward where you left your shoes and stockings. Pick up that sea shell you see lying in the sand just ahead of you and put it to your ear and listen to the message from the shell.

PAUSE 5 SECONDS

Now turn and look at the sea once more and say "good-bye." It is time to return to put on your shoes and stockings . . . go back up the stairs of life . . . to the top of the rock. You have the love and excitement of life drawn up from the sea within you now. Say a special thanks to those people who have been thoughtful to you as your sea fades from view.

You have just experienced an altered state of consciousness that put you into balance mentally and spiritually. You have been given a valuable tool to use to enrich your life. Use it every day and design your life the way you want it to be. At this moment you are making a commitment to yourself. A commitment to keep yourself free of all negativism from now on and to make your entire life a positive, happy, fulfilling experience. The choice is yours alone to do or not to do. For you are in control now. And whatever you choose to do, you can do. Whatever you set your own mind to achieve, you can and will achieve it. You will be completely successful and you will enjoy your success. And you will enjoy being the positive, worthwhile person you really want to be more and more every day.

The next time you hear my voice you will allow yourself to relax ten times more deeply relaxed than you are now, and the suggestions I give you then will go ten times deeper into every level of your mind.

In a few moments when you awaken yourself, you will feel very, very relaxed and you will feel completely refreshed, alive, alert, full of energy and full of self-confidence. You will feel simply marvelous. All you have to do to awaken is to count with me from one up to five and at the count of five you will awaken feeling relaxed, refreshed, alert, and in very high spirits. Feeling very good indeed. 1 . . . 2 . . . 3 . . . 4 . . . 5. Open eyes, wide awake, feeling just great!

● ● ●

Weight and Diet Control

THIS TAPE will guide you into an altered state of consciousness that will enable you to control your diet and your weight. This tape assumes that you have a weight problem due to improper eating habits and can help you solve that problem if you really want to have improved eating habits and an improved weight distribution for your body. However, this tape cannot make you do anything you really do not want to do. If you really and truly want to establish a nutritious diet, and really want to adjust your weight to a healthy level, then proceed with this tape.

One caution. This is not a medical program and does not purport to be a medical program. This tape has to do with willpower, self-image, and balance in eating habits. It is a habit control tape. Therefore, if your weight problem is due to medical reasons such as thyroid malfunctioning or other such physical conditions, do not use this tape unless your medical practitioner says it is all right to do so. Take your medical problems to your medical practitioner. Use this tape only for what it is intended—habit control.

In this Weight and Diet Control tape script there is a specific diet included. This specific diet is for illustration purposes only and may not be the best or correct diet for you. *In the script where this diet is given you should substitute the correct diet for yourself; consult your medical practitioner or a nutritionist if necessary.* The sample diet in this tape script is not intended to be a medically sound diet for everyone. It is your responsibility to determine your own diet and substitute it in this tape script.

There are two ways you can use this tape—either all by itself or in conjunction with the Goal Setting and Willpower tape (see Chapter 13).

If you use this diet control tape by itself, listen to it at least once every day and follow the instructions and suggestions until you have reached your weight goal. Then you may stop listening to the tape and maintain the weight you want.

If you use this tape in conjunction with the Goal Setting and Willpower tape, alternate between the tapes. One day use the diet tape, the next day use the Goal Setting and Willpower tape. Then the diet tape the following day, and so forth.

For the Goal Setting and Willpower tape, you would write out and program your goal something like this: *I want to follow a strict, healthy diet that will allow me to lose the proper amount of weight that is best for me. Then I want to maintain a proper, healthy weight level from that point on.* Or you can devise some other wording of your goal that you think is best for you.

Weight and Diet Control Tape Script

Close your eyes and take a nice deep, full breath and exhale completely, all the way to the bottom of your lungs. All out. Do it again now. Just relax and let it all out. One more time, and this time hold your breath when you have filled your lungs with clean, refreshing, relaxing air. Hold it in. Keep your eyes closed. Now let your breath out slowly and feel yourself relaxing all over.

I want you to imagine now that all your tensions, all your tightness, and all your fears and worries are draining away from the top of your head. Let it drain down through your face, down through your neck, through your shoulders, through your chest, your waist, your hips, your thighs, down through your knees, your calves, your ankles, your feet, and out your toes. All your tension, all your tightness, all your worries and fears are draining away now from the very tips of your toes, and you are relaxing more and more.

Focus your attention on your toes now and allow your toes to relax completely. Each toe is loose and heavy. Now let this relaxation flow into your feet, into your ankles, your calves, your knees. Feel it flowing into your thighs, into your hips, into your waist, flowing up into your chest now. Feel your breathing easier and deeper, more regular and more relaxed. Now let the deep relaxed feeling go into your shoulders, down your arms, into your upper arms, your forearms, and into your hands and fingers, and flowing back into your forearms, your upper arms, your shoulders. Flowing into your neck, over your face, your chin, your cheeks, even your ears are relaxed. Feel it flowing into your eyes and eyelids now. Your eyelids are so heavy and smooth. Flowing up into your eyebrows, over your forehead, over the top of your head, down the back of your head, and down the back of your neck.

A new heaviness is starting in your toes now. Twice as heavy as the first time. Imagine a heavy weight on each toe. Feel the heaviness deep and even more relaxed. And this heavy, deep feeling is going into your feet, your ankles, your calves, your knees, going into your thighs, your hips, into your waist. Flowing up into your chest now, relaxing your heart, relaxing your lungs, allowing your breathing to be more intense, more regular, more and more completely relaxed. Now the deep heavy feeling is flowing into your shoulders, and down your arms, your upper arms, your forearms, into your hands and fingers. And now flowing back through your forearms, your upper arms, into your shoulders and into your neck. Flowing over your face, into your eyes, over your eyebrows, over your forehead, over the top of your head, down the back of your head, and down the back of your neck.

And a new heaviness is starting now at the top of your head. Twice as heavy as before. Twice as heavy. Imagine a heavy weight on the very top of your head, soft and relaxed and heavy. Feel the heavy relaxation flowing down into your face and eyes now, down through your neck, your shoulders, flowing down through your chest, your waist, your hips, your thighs, your knees, into your calves, your ankles, your feet and toes. Deeply relaxed, loose and limp, and comfortable from the top of your head to the very tip of your toes.

I want you to imagine now that you are looking at a blackboard. On the blackboard imagine a circle. Into the circle we are going to place the letters of the alphabet in reverse order, and with each letter after you place it into the circle, you will erase it then from inside the circle and allow yourself to relax more and more deeply.

Picture the blackboard now. Picture the circle. Into the circle put the letter Z. Now erase the Z from inside the circle, and go deeper. Put Y into the circle, and go deeper. X, and erase it and go deeper. W, and erase it. V, and erase it. U, and erase it. T, and erase it. S, and erase it. R, and erase it. Q, and erase it. P, and erase it. O, and erase it. N, and erase it. M, and erase it. L, and erase it. K, and erase it. J, and erase it. I, and erase it. H, and erase it. G, and erase it. F, and erase it. E, and erase it. D, and erase it. C, and erase it. B, and erase it. A, and erase it. Now erase the circle and forget about the blackboard. Just go on relaxing more and more deeply. Feel yourself sink into the chair, mind and body drifting deeper and deeper into relaxation, deeper with each breath.

I want you to imagine now that you are looking at a clear, blue summer sky. And in the sky, a skywriting airplane is writing your first name in fluffy, white cloudlike letters. See your name floating fluffy, white, and cloudlike in a clear, blue sky. Now let your name just dissolve away. Let the winds just blow your name away into the blue. Forget about your name. Forget you even have a name. Names are not important. Just go on listening to my voice and allowing yourself to relax more deeply.

I want you to imagine now that I am placing on each of your knees a heavy bag of sand. Feel the sand pressing down on your knees. Your knees are growing heavier and more relaxed. In the sand is a very powerful numbing ingredient and the numbness is flowing down into your knees now. Your knees are growing numb and more numb under the sand. And the heavy, numb feeling is flowing down into your calves, into your ankles, into your feet and toes. Everything below your knees is numb and more numb from the sand. And now the heavy, numb feeling is going up into your thighs, flowing into your hips, through your waist, and into your chest. It flows into your shoulders, and they grow numb and heavy. It flows down your arms, your upper arms, your forearms, into your hands and fingers. Flowing back now through your forearms, your upper arms, your shoulders, and into your neck. Over your face, your eyes. Flowing up to your eyebrows, your forehead, over the top of your head, down the back of your head, and down the back of your neck.

As you go on floating, drifting smoothly and gently, more and more deeply relaxed with each breath, I want you to focus your attention on the very tip of your nose. Keep your attention focused gently and lazily on the tip of your nose until you reach a point where your entire attention is on the sound of my voice. And when you reach that point, you can forget about your nose and just go on listening to my voice and allowing yourself to relax more and more deeply. As you keep your attention gently focused on the tip of your nose, I want you to imagine . . . imagine that I am placing on your tongue, in your mouth, a small bite of chocolate candy. You don't swallow it; it just sits there on your tongue. Notice the bitter taste of the chocolate. It is bitter and it is growing more bitter and more bitter as it just sits there, melting on your tongue. It is so bitter that you can hardly keep it in your mouth. It tastes terrible. From now on you will be completely free from any desire for chocolate or candy or sweet foods of any kind. You will be completely free from that desire, completely free from now on. I am taking the bitter chocolate from your mouth now. Your mouth feels clean now, all fresh and clean. You are glad that that ugly taste is gone from your tongue.

I want you to imagine now that you are standing on the top step of a heavy wooden staircase. Feel the carpet under your feet. The carpet can be any kind and color you wish . . . create it. Now extend your hand out and touch the railing. Feel the smooth polished wood of the railing under your hand. You are standing just ten steps up from the floor below. The stairs are curving very smoothly down to the floor below. In a moment we will walk down the stairs. With each step down you will allow yourself to relax even more deeply. By the time you reach the floor below you will be deeper than you have ever gone before. Take a step down now, down to the ninth step smoothly and easily. Feel yourself going deeper. Now down to eight, deeper still. Now down to seven . . . six . . . five . . . four . . . three . . . two . . . one. Now you are standing on the floor below. There is a door in front of you. Reach out and open the door. And from the room beyond the door a flood of light comes streaming out through the open doorway. Walk into the room, into the light through the open door. You are inside the room now, look around you. This is your room, and it can be anything you want it to be.

Any size, any shape, any colors. You can have anything in this room that you want. You can add things, remove things, rearrange things. You can have any kind of furniture, fixtures, paintings, windows, carpets, or whatever you want because this is your place…your very own private inner place and you are free here. Free to create, free to be who you are. Free to do whatever you will, and the light that shines in this room is your light. Feel the light all around you, shining on the beautiful things in your room. Shining on you; feel the energy in the light. Let the light flow all through your body now. Going in through every pore in your skin. Filling you completely. Pushing away all doubt. Pushing out all fear and tension. You are filled with the light. You are clear and radiant, glowing with the shining light in your room.

While you are standing in the light in your room, I want you to build an image. An image of yourself as you really want to be. Not as someone else wants you to be, but as you really want yourself to be. See your image standing in front of you in the light. Your image is trim, healthy, attractive, calm and free, wearing well-fitting clothes that look so fine on your nicely proportioned body. This is you. This is the real you. This is the person you are now becoming. Walk closer to your image now. Walk closer. Now walk into the image. Let it blend into your very body. Your own best self, a living part of you now.

At this moment you are making yourself a promise—a commitment to become the real you. This commitment will be with you, stronger every day.

From now on, every day you will be more and more completely the person you really want to be. You will be relaxed and calm. And no matter what is going on around you, you can handle it in a relaxed and sensible manner. And you will feel so good. You will have all the energy you can use every single day. And it will be so easy to stay on your diet strictly every day no matter where you are no matter what you are doing.

In the morning you will have a small serving of protein, a small serving of fruit or juice and one piece of toast served without butter. For lunch you will have one small serving of protein and a small serving of fresh fruit or vegetable. For dinner you will have a small dinner salad with a very light dressing, a small serving of protein and one half cup of cooked vegetable served without butter or margarine.

You will always eat very slowly, and when you have eaten just a little bit of the proper, sensible foods you will feel full, completely full and satisfied on just a little bit of the right foods. That is all your body needs now, and that is all you will want. You will have no desire at all to nibble or snack between meals or after dinner. You will have no desire at all for sweets or starches or rich greasy foods of any kind. All that is in the past for you now. Your body does not need that, and you do not even want it. For you are now forming the habit of eating correctly for your body. And your body is adjusting to this habit more and more completely every day. As your stomach continues to shrink a little bit every day, you will feel full and comfortable on less and less food. And your weight will keep on going down, even faster than before, so fast and easy. Every day you will keep on becoming more trim, healthy, and attractive. And you will feel simply marvelous every day.

Each time you listen to this tape you will become ten times more deeply relaxed than before and the suggestions you receive on this tape will be stronger and go deeper all the time. For you are in control now. Whatever you choose to do, you can do. Whatever you set your mind to achieve, you can and will achieve. You will be completely successful, and you will enjoy your success. And you will enjoy becoming more and more trim and attractive every day. You will enjoy feeling healthy and more and more your real self every day.

In a moment, I am going to count backward from 10 to 1. I want you to count with me silently to yourself. Think each number as I say it, and allow each number to take you deeper. 10 . . . 9 . . . 8 . . . 7 . . . 6 . . . 5 . . . 4 . . . 3 . . . 2 . . . 1. You are now very deeply relaxed. You can give yourself the following suggestions. Say the words to yourself with me as I say them.

I will always be relaxed and calm.

I will not want anything to eat between meals, and I will not eat in between meals.

I will eat only at regular mealtimes, and even then I will eat only small, balanced portions of nutritious foods. And all the calories in the foods I do eat will be completely utilized by my body and not be stored as fat.

I will strictly follow the diet I prescribe for myself, and this is so.

Now take a deep breath and relax.

The next time you hear my voice on tape, you will allow yourself to relax even more completely than you are now. And the suggestions you have received on this tape will keep on going deeper and deeper and deeper into every level of your mind.

In a few moments when you awaken yourself, you will feel very, very relaxed, and you will be completely refreshed, alive, alert, full of energy, full of confidence. You will feel simply marvelous. All you have to do to awaken is to count with me from one up to five and at the count of five, open your eyes, feeling relaxed, refreshed, alert, in very high spirits. Feeling very good indeed. 1 . . . 2 . . . 3 . . . 4 . . . 5.

● ● ●

General Relaxation and Stress Control

THIS SELF-HYPNOSIS tape is excellent to use anytime you wish to relax, to relieve stress or tension, and to just make yourself feel great. This tape is also excellent to use prior to using any other hypnosis tape in order to better condition yourself for excellent hypnosis results. You may use this tape as often as you wish. I recommend that you use it at least once a week just to maintain better control of your life.

Relaxation Tape Script

Close your eyes and take a deep, full breath and exhale completely, all the way to the bottom of your lungs. All out. Do it again now. Just relax and let it all out. One more time, and this time hold your breath when you have filled your lungs with clean, refreshing, relaxing air. Hold it in. Keep your eyes closed. Now let your breath out slowly and feel yourself relaxing all over.

Focus your attention on your knees now and relax everything below your knees. Relax your calves. Relax your ankles. Relax your feet. And relax your toes. Relax your toes. Everything below your knees is now loose and relaxed. Now relax your thighs as completely as you can. Let your thighs just droop limp and loose and heavy into the chair. Relax your hips and relax your waist. Now relax your chest as completely as you can. Allow your breathing to be easier and deeper, more regular and more relaxed. Relax your shoulders now. Let the muscles in your shoulders be heavy and loose. More and more completely relaxed. Relax your neck and throat. Let your head just droop as all the muscles in your neck just relax. Now relax your face as completely as you can. Allow your face to be smooth and loose, relaxed and easy, your jaws all loose and relaxed, your teeth not quite touching. Everything smooth and loose and easy. Now relax as completely as you can all the little muscles around your eyelids. Feel your eyelids growing heavier and smoother. More and more deeply relaxed.

I want you to imagine now that all your tensions, all your tightness, and all your fears and worries are draining away from the top of your head. Let it drain down through your face, down through your neck, through your shoulders, through your chest, your waist, your hips, your thighs, down through your knees, your calves, your ankles, your feet, and out your toes. All your tension, all your tightness, all your worries and fears are draining away now from the very tips of your toes, and you are relaxing more and more.

We are going to do this relaxation exercise again. This

time I want you to allow yourself to relax even more fully and completely than you did the first time.

Focus your attention on your knees once again and relax everything below your knees. Relax your calves. Relax your ankles. Relax your feet, and relax your toes. And now relax your thighs even more completely. Allow your thighs to droop limp and heavy into the chair. Relax your hips and your waist. Feel the relaxation flowing into your chest now. Relaxing the vital organs within your chest, your heart, your lungs, allowing your breathing to be more intense, more regular, more and more completely relaxed. Now relax your shoulders even more. Feel your shoulders heavy and loose. More and more deeply relaxed. Relax your neck and throat. Relax your face even more. Feel your face all smooth and loose, completely easy and relaxed all over. And now relax even more all the little muscles around your eyelids. Feel your eyelids heavy and smooth, more and more deeply relaxed.

We are going to do this relaxation exercise once again. This time I want you to allow yourself to relax completely. There is nothing to fear, you will always hear me, so just pull out all the stops and allow yourself to sink into perfect relaxation.

Focus your attention again on your knees and relax everything below your knees. Relax your calves, relax your ankles, relax your feet, and relax your toes. Now relax your thighs completely. Feel the deep and heavy relaxation flowing into your hips now. Feel it going up through your waist, flowing into your chest, to your shoulders, heavy and loose, completely relaxed. And now this heavy relaxed feeling is going into your neck and throat, all over your face. Your face is all smooth and loose, completely easy and relaxed, and the heavy relaxation is flowing into your eyes and eyelids now. Your eyelids are so heavy and so smooth. Ever more deeply relaxed.

I want you to imagine now that you are looking at a blackboard. And on the blackboard is a circle. Into the circle put the letter X. Now erase the X from inside the circle. And now erase the circle. Forget about the blackboard now as you just go on relaxing more and more deeply.

In a moment, I am going to count backwards from 100. I want you to count with me silently to yourself. Say each number to yourself as I say it, then when I ask you, erase the number from your mind and allow yourself to relax even more deeply. 100 . . . say the 100 to yourself. Now erase it from your mind and go deeper. 99 . . . and erase it all away. 98 and erase it. 97 and now erase it so completely there is nothing left at all, just deeper and deeper waves of relaxation.

Focus your attention now on the very tip of your nose. Keep your attention gently focused on the tip of your nose until you reach a point where your entire attention is on my voice. And when you reach that point, you can forget about your nose and just go on listening to my voice and allowing yourself to relax more and more deeply. And as you keep your attention focused very gently on the tip of your nose I am going to take you down through four progressively deeper levels of relaxation.

I will label these levels with letters of the alphabet, and when you reach the first level, level A, you will be ten times more deeply relaxed than you are even now. And then from level A we will go down to level B, and when you reach level B you will be ten times again more deeply relaxed than you were before. And from level B we will go down even further, down to level C. And when you reach level C you will be ten times again more deeply relaxed than before. And then from level C we will go all the way down to the deepest level of relaxation, level D. And when you reach level D, you will be ten times again more deeply relaxed than before. You are drifting down now, two times deeper with each breath that you exhale. Two times deeper with each breath. Your hands and fingers are so relaxed and heavy, and they keep growing heavier. Feel the heaviness growing in your hands and fingers. Heavy...heavier...heavier still until now they are so heavy it is as though your hands and fingers were made of lead. And this deep relaxed, heavy feeling is flowing up through your forearms now. Feel it going up into your upper arms. Flowing through your shoulders, into your neck, over your face, over your eyes. Flowing up to your eyebrows, your forehead, over the top of your head. The deep relaxed, heavy feeling is flowing down the back of your head and down the back of your neck. You are now approaching level A.

You are on level A now and still going deeper. Five times deeper now with each breath that you exhale. Five times deeper with each breath. Your mind is so still and peaceful. You're not thinking of anything now.

Too relaxed to think. Too comfortable to think. And this heavy relaxation in your mind is flowing into your face and eyes. It is flowing down through your neck and into your chest. Flowing down to your waist, down through your hips, your thighs, your knees, your calves, your ankles, your feet and your toes. You are now approaching level B.

You are on level B now and still drifting deeper. Floating smoothly and gently into perfect relaxation. Your arms and legs are so relaxed and heavy they feel like logs. Your arms and legs are stiff and numb and heavy . . . simply immovable. Your arms and legs are like planks of wood. You are now approaching level C.

You are on level C now and still drifting down. Sinking into the chair. Sinking deeper and deeper into perfect relaxation. And as you go on drifting even deeper, I am going to count backwards from 15 to 1. Each number that I say will take you deeper and deeper still, and when I reach 1 you will be on level D. 15, deeper, 14, deeper still, 13 . . . 12 . . . 11 . . . 10 . . . 9 . . . 8 . . . 7 . . . 6, let it all go now, 5 . . . 4 . . . 3 . . . 2 . . . 1 . . . 1 . . . 1, so deep, so dreamy, so heavy, so misty.

You are now on level D and still drifting down. There is no limit now . . . no limit. Go on floating, drifting deeper and deeper into perfect relaxation, deeper with each breath.

As you continue to drift deeper and deeper into perfect relaxation, I offer these suggestions for your benefit.

Using this and other hypnosis tapes or practicing your own self-hypnosis enables you to get more control of your life and to enrich your life by solving your problems.

These states of deep relaxation are very beneficial to your mental and physical health.

You are now becoming more relaxed, and you will continue to be more relaxed every day. You will always be relaxed and calm no matter what is happening around you. And anything that does happen, you can handle it in a relaxed, mature, and sensible manner. For you are now learning to be more and more in control of your own life. You will no longer allow other people or events to intimidate you or to cause you stress. You are in control, and you like it that way. You will be calm, relaxed, confident, and in control at all times.

You are learning to relax...to release all anxiety and relax and let go. For you are in control of all aspects of your life now. No longer will you allow anxiety, tension, or nervous energy to impede you. Every day you will notice yourself relaxing more. You will notice yourself becoming more calm and more in control than ever before.

You will notice every day that your attitude is becoming more and more philosophical and free of serious concern about life's daily problems.

You will feel very relaxed, yet very alert.

Now repeat the following suggestion to yourself as I say it, "Every day in every way I am getting better, better, and better."

Now, take a deep breath and relax.

The next time you hear my voice on tape, you will allow yourself to relax ten times more deeply relaxed than you are now. And the suggestions I give you then will go ten times deeper into your mind.

In a few moments I will awaken you. When you awaken you will feel very relaxed and very refreshed all over. You will feel alive and alert, very refreshed. Full of energy. You will feel just wonderful. You will keep on feeling relaxed and fine all the rest of today, and all this evening. Tonight when you are ready to go to sleep, you will sleep just like a log all night long. And the first thing you know it will be morning, and you will awaken feeling on top of the world.

I am now going to count from 1 to 5. At the count of 5 you will open your eyes, be wide awake and feeling fine, feeling relaxed, refreshed, alert, and in very high spirits. Feeling simply terrific!

1 . . . 2 . . . coming up slowly now . . . 3 . . . at the count of 5 you will open your eyes, be wide awake and feeling fine, feeling better than before . . . 4 . . . 5.

SNAP FINGERS

Open eyes, wide awake and feeling fine, feeling better than before, and this is so!

● ● ●

18

Self-Image Improvement

WITH THIS tape you are going to enter into an altered state of consciousness that will enable you to improve your self-image by creating the image of yourself as you really want to be and then taking the steps to make that image become reality in the physical world.

I suggest that you take a few minutes, or hours if necessary, to seriously think about what you really want for yourself. Do you want more confidence? Would you like to be more outgoing? In better health? Have a new job? Be more patient? Be more decisive? Be free of negative thoughts and actions?

Think about all aspects of what and who you really want to be. Write it down and study it if necessary. Have the image of yourself as you really want to be in your mind. This tape will help you turn that image into reality.

Do not be concerned that you must get everything done in one session of listening to this tape. You can change or modify your self-image anytime you wish by listening to this tape as often as you wish and making whatever changes you wish. This tape is not a one-time thing; it is designed to give you a tool to use every day for the rest of your life, enriching your life in whatever way you choose.

Self-Image
Tape Script

Close your eyes and take a deep, full breath and exhale completely, all the way to the bottom of your lungs. All out. Do it again now. Just relax and let it all out. One more time, and this time hold your breath when you have filled your lungs with clean, refreshing, relaxing air. Hold it in. Keep your eyes closed. Now let your breath out slowly and feel yourself relaxing all over.

I want you to imagine now that all your tensions, all your tightness, and all your fears and worries are draining away from the top of your head. Let it drain down through your face, down through your neck, through your shoulders, through your chest, your waist, your hips, your thighs, down through your knees, your calves, your ankles, your feet, and out your toes. All your tension, all your tightness, all your worries and fears are draining away now from the very tips of your toes, and you are relaxing more and more.

Focus your attention on your toes now and allow your toes to relax completely. Each toe is loose and heavy. Now let this relaxation flow into your feet, into your ankles, your calves, your knees. Feel it flowing into your thighs, into your hips, into your waist, flowing up into your chest now. Feel your breathing easier and deeper, more regular and more relaxed. Now let the deep relaxed feeling go into your shoulders, down your arms, into your upper arms, your forearms, and into your hands and fingers, and flowing back into your forearms, your upper arms, your shoulders.

Flowing into your neck, over your face, your chin, your cheeks, even your ears are relaxed. Feel it flowing into your eyes and eyelids now. Your eyelids are so heavy and smooth. Flowing up into your eyebrows, over your forehead, over the top of your head, down the back of your head, and down the back of your neck.

A new heaviness is starting in your toes now. Twice as heavy as the first time. Imagine a heavy weight on each toe. Feel the heaviness deep and even more relaxed. And this heavy, deep feeling is going into your feet, your ankles, your calves, your knees, going into your thighs, your hips, into your waist. Flowing up into your chest now, relaxing your heart, relaxing your lungs, allowing your breathing to be more intense, more regular, more and more completely relaxed. Now the deep heavy feeling is flowing into your shoulders, and down your arms, your upper arms, your forearms, into your hands and fingers. And now flowing back through your forearms, your upper arms, into your shoulders and into your neck. Flowing over your face, into your eyes, over your eyebrows, over your forehead, over the top of your head, down the back of your head and down the back of your neck.

And a new heaviness is starting now at the top of your head. Twice as heavy as before. Twice as heavy. Imagine a heavy weight on the very top of your head, soft and relaxed and heavy. Feel the heavy relaxation flowing down into your face and eyes now, down through your neck, your shoulders, flowing down through your chest, your waist, your hips, your thighs, your knees, into your calves, your ankles, your feet and toes. Deeply relaxed, loose and limp, and comfortable from the top of your head to the very tip of your toes.

I want you to imagine now that you are looking at a blackboard. On the blackboard imagine a circle. Into the circle we are going to place the letters of the alphabet in reverse order, and with each letter after you place it into the circle, you will erase it then from inside the circle and allow yourself to relax more and more deeply.

Picture the blackboard now. Picture the circle. Into the circle put the letter Z. Now erase the Z from inside the circle, and go deeper. Put Y into the circle, and erase it and go deeper. X, and erase it and go deeper still. W, and erase it. V, and erase it. U, and erase it. T, and erase it. S, and erase it. R, and erase it. Q, and erase it. P, and erase it. O, and erase it. N, and erase it. M, and erase it. L, and erase it. K, and erase it. J, and erase it. I, and erase it. H, and erase it. G, and erase it. F, and erase it. E, and erase it. D, and erase it. C, and erase it. B, and erase it. A, and erase it. Now erase the circle and forget about the blackboard. Just go on relaxing more and more deeply. Feel yourself sink into the chair, mind and body drifting deeper and deeper into relaxation, deeper with each breath.

As you breathe in, imagine that you are breathing in a pure, clean, odorless anesthesia. The anesthesia is flowing all throughout your body now. It is a warm, numb, tingling feeling, and the more you breathe in, the more you want to breathe in, and you allow your breathing to become even deeper now, bringing in more and more of this peaceful, relaxing, tranquil feeling.

From now on until the end of this session, you will allow yourself to relax more and more completely with each breath you take.

I want you to imagine now that you are looking at a clear, blue summer sky. And in the sky, a skywriting airplane is writing your first name in fluffy, white cloud-like letters. See your name floating fluffy, white, and cloudlike in a clear, blue sky. Now let your name just dissolve away. Let the winds just blow your name away into the blue. Forget about your name. Forget you even have a name. Names are not important. Just go on listening to my voice and allowing yourself to relax more deeply.

I want you to imagine now that you are standing on the top step of a heavy wooden staircase. Feel the carpet under your feet. The carpet can be any kind and color you wish, create it. Now extend your hand out and touch the railing.

Feel the smooth polished wood of the railing under your hand. You are standing just ten steps up from the floor below. The stairs are curving very smoothly down to the floor below. In a moment we will walk down the stairs. With each step down you will allow yourself to relax even more deeply. By the time you reach the floor below you will be deeper than you have ever gone before. Take a step down now, down to the ninth step smoothly and easily. Feel yourself going deeper.

Now down to eight, deeper still. Now down to seven . . . six . . . five . . . four . . . three . . . two . . . one. Now you are standing on the floor below. There is a door in front of you. Reach out and open the door.

And from the room beyond the door a flood of light comes streaming out through the open doorway. Walk into the room, into the light through the open door. You are inside the room now, look around you. This is your room, and it can be anything you want it to be.

Any size, any shape, any colors. You can have anything in this room that you want. You can add things, remove things, rearrange things. You can have any kind of furniture, fixtures, paintings, windows, carpets, or whatever you want because this is your place ... your very own private inner place and you are free here. Free to create, free to be who you are. Free to do whatever you will, and the light that shines in this room is your light. Feel the light all around you, shining on the beautiful things in your room. Shining on you, feel the energy in the light. Let the light flow all through your body now. Going in through every pore in your skin. Filling you completely. Pushing away all doubt. Pushing out all fear and tension. You are filled with the light. You are clear and radiant, glowing with the shining light in your room.

While you are standing in the light in your room, I want you to build an image. An image of yourself as you really want to be. Not as someone else wants you to be, but as you really want yourself to be. See your image standing in front of you in the light. See the quiet look of confidence on the face of your image. Notice the healthy trim body. Notice how calm and free your image is. I will stop talking now for two minutes while you give your image all the qualities and attributes you wish it to have.

PAUSE 120 SECONDS

Now take a final look at your image. This is you. This is the real you. This is the person you are now becoming. Walk closer to your image now. Walk closer. Now walk into your image. Let it blend into your very body. Your own best self, a living part of you now. Stronger every day.

From now on, every day you will be more and more completely the person you really want to be. You will be relaxed and calm. And no matter what is going on around you, you can handle it in a relaxed and sensible manner. And you will feel so good. You will have all the energy you can use every single day. And it will be so easy for you to stay in complete control of every aspect of your life. You will find it very easy to dispel all fears, anxieties, doubts, and troubles. You are in total control of your life, and this is so.

Now take one final look around your room. You can come back here anytime you wish. You can come here for any purpose you wish . . . to pray . . . to consult with higher mind . . . to set goals . . . to meditate . . . to create . . . to learn . . . to solve problems...to make changes to your self-image.

What you do in your room has no limit. No limit.

You have just experienced using the altered state of consciousness to go deep within self to a private, powerful, creative place that you can use for practical purposes and for spiritual purposes. You have been given this valuable tool to use to enrich your life. Use it every day and design your life the way you want it to be. The choice is yours alone to do or not to do, for you are in control now. And whatever you choose to do, you can do. Whatever you set your own mind to achieve, you can and will achieve it. You will be completely successful and you will enjoy your success. And you will enjoy becoming the person you really want to be more and more every day.

The next time you hear my voice on tape, you will allow yourself to relax ten times more deeply relaxed than you are now. And the suggestions I give you then will go ten times deeper into your mind.

In a few moments when you awaken yourself, you will feel very, very relaxed and you will feel completely refreshed, alive, alert, full of energy and full of self-confidence. You will feel simply marvelous. All you have to do to awaken yourself is to count with me from one up to five and at the count of five you will awaken feeling relaxed, refreshed, alert, and in very high spirits. Feeling very good indeed. 1 . . . 2 . . . 3 . . . 4 . . . 5. Open eyes, wide awake and feeling fine, feeling better than before, and this is so!

●　　●　　●

Smoking Habit Control

19

THIS TAPE will direct you into an altered state of consciousness that can enable you to get rid of your smoking habit if you really want to. If you really want to continue smoking but have decided to give it up because of someone else, this tape will not do the job for you. Self-hypnosis can enable you to do anything that you really want to do, but it is not able to force you to do something that you really do not want to do.

You should listen to this tape at least once every day until you have succeeded in eliminating your smoking habit. If for some reason you are unable to listen every day, be sure to use the tape at least once every week. If you allow more than one week to lapse between sessions, you may not get the results you want because post-hypnotic suggestion weakens in one to two weeks.

After you have stopped smoking, you need not listen to the tape anymore. If after you quit smoking you get the urge to start again, then get out the tape and listen to it. Use the tape as necessary to continue being a non-smoker.

Smoking Control
Tape Script

Close your eyes and take a deep, full breath and exhale completely, all the way to the bottom of your lungs. All out. Do it again now. Just relax and let it all out. One more time, and this time hold your breath when you have filled your lungs with clean, refreshing, relaxing air. Hold it in. Keep your eyes closed. Now let your breath out slowly and feel yourself relaxing all over.

Focus your attention on your toes now and allow your toes to relax completely. Each toe is loose and heavy. Now let this relaxation flow into your feet, into your ankles, your calves, your knees. Feel it flowing into your thighs, into your hips, into your waist, flowing up into your chest now. Feel your breathing easier and deeper, more regular and more relaxed. Now let the deep relaxed feeling go into your shoulders, down your arms, into your upper arms, your forearms, and into your hands and fingers, and flowing back into your forearms, your upper arms, your shoulders. Flowing into your neck, over your face, your chin, your cheeks, even your ears are relaxed. Feel it flowing into your eyes and eyelids now. Your eyelids are so heavy and smooth. Flowing up into your eyebrows, over your forehead, over the top of your head, down the back of your head, and down the back of your neck.

A new heaviness is starting in your toes now. Twice as heavy as the first time. Imagine a heavy weight on each toe. Feel the heaviness deep and even more relaxed. And this heavy, deep feeling is going into your feet, your ankles, your calves, your knees, going into your thighs, your hips, into your waist. Flowing up into your chest now, relaxing your heart, relaxing your lungs, allowing your breathing to be more intense, more regular, more and more completely relaxed. Now the deep, heavy feeling is flowing into your shoulders, and down your arms, your upper arms, your forearms, into your hands and fingers. And now flowing back through your forearms, your upper arms, into your shoulders and into your neck. Flowing over your face, into your eyes, over your eyebrows, over your forehead, over the top of your head, down the back of your head and down the back of your neck.

And a new heaviness is starting now at the top of your head. Twice as heavy as before. Twice as heavy. Imagine a heavy weight on the very top of your head, soft and relaxed and heavy. Feel the heavy relaxation flowing down into your face and eyes now, down through your neck, your shoulders, flowing down through your chest, your waist, your hips, your thighs, your knees, into your calves, your ankles, your feet and toes. Deeply relaxed, loose and limp, and comfortable from the top of your head to the very tip of your toes.

I want you to imagine now that you are looking at a blackboard. On the blackboard imagine a circle. Into the circle we are going to place the letters of the alphabet in reverse order, and with each letter after you place it into the circle, you will erase it then from inside the circle and allow yourself to relax more and more deeply.

Picture the blackboard now. Picture the circle. Into the circle put the letter Z. Now erase the Z from inside the circle, and go deeper. Put Y into the circle, and erase it and go deeper. X, and erase it and go deeper still. W, and erase it. V, and erase it. U, and erase it. T, and erase it. S, and erase it. R, and erase it. Q, and erase it. P, and erase it. O, and erase it. N, and erase it. M, and erase it. L, and erase it. K, and erase it. J, and erase it. I, and erase it. H, and erase it. G, and erase it. F, and erase it. E, and erase it. D, and erase it. C, and erase it. B, and erase it. A, and erase it. Now erase the circle and forget about the blackboard. Just go on relaxing more and more deeply. Feel yourself sink into the chair, mind and body drifting deeper and deeper into relaxation, deeper with each breath.

I want you to imagine now that you are looking at a clear, blue summer sky. And in the sky, a skywriting airplane is writing your first name in fluffy, white cloudlike letters. See your name floating fluffy, white, and cloudlike in a clear, blue sky. Now let your name just dissolve away. Let the winds just blow your name away into the blue. Forget about your name. Forget you even have a name. Names are not important. Just go on listening to my voice and allowing yourself to relax more deeply.

I want you to imagine now that I am placing on each of your knees a heavy bag of sand. Feel the sand pressing down on your knees. Your knees are growing heavier and more relaxed. In the sand is a very powerful numbing ingredient and the numbness is flowing down into your knees now. Your knees are growing numb and more numb under the sand. And the heavy, numb feeling is flowing down into your calves, into your ankles, into your feet and toes. Everything below your knees is numb and more numb from the sand. And now the heavy, numb feeling is going up into your thighs, flowing into your hips, through your waist, and into your chest. It flows into your shoulders, and they grow numb and heavy. It flows down your arms, your upper arms, your forearms, into your hands and fingers. Flowing back now through your forearms, your upper arms, your shoulders, and into your neck. Over your face, your eyes. Flowing up to your eyebrows, your forehead, over the top of your head, down the back of your head, and down the back of your neck.

As you go on floating, drifting smoothly and gently, more and more deeply relaxed with each breath, I want you to focus your attention on the very tip of your nose. Keep your attention focused gently and lazily on the tip of your nose until you reach a point where your entire attention is on the sound of my voice. And when you reach that point, you can forget about your nose and just go on listening to my voice and allowing yourself to relax more and more deeply. As you keep your attention gently focused on the tip of your nose, I want you to imagine now that you are lighting a cigarette. Put the cigarette in your mouth. You try to draw in a lung full of the smoke, but the taste is so bad that you immediately blow the smoke out. A foul taste still lingers on your tongue. Your tongue tastes like you have been licking the inside of a dirty, black, crusty, filthy chimney. The taste is growing more bitter and more bitter as it just sits there coating your tongue. It is so bitter that you cannot stand to leave it in your mouth. It tastes terrible. From now on you will be completely free from any desire for cigarettes or tobacco of any kind. You will be completely free from that desire, completely free from now on. Now take a cup of mouthwash and rinse your mouth thoroughly. One rinse helps, but even that is not enough to get rid of all the foul taste. Rinse again and again. Now your mouth feels clean . . . all fresh and clean. You are glad that that ugly taste is gone from your tongue.

Now look down at the burning cigarette still in your hand. The smoke drifts up into your nostrils and you are keenly aware of its dirty, stuffy, burning smell. It smells as bad as it tasted. The smell chokes you and irritates your throat. You realize that this smell has impregnated your hair and skin and clothing. It makes you smell like the inside of a filthy chimney. You must smell that way to other people, too. And the smoke must have made your house and car smell foul and dirty, also. You realize now that you have created an image of yourself as that of a smelly, dirty person. You realize also that you were inconsiderate of others by fouling up their air and their environment.

You don't even want to be associated with this cigarette or any other cigarette. Take the cigarette now and crush it out completely in an ashtray. Now throw the ashtray into a garbage can.

Now wash your hands with clean, fragrant soap. Get a can of air deodorizer and spray the air to get rid of the foul cigarette odor.

Look into a mirror now. See how much better you look already. That is because you feel better about yourself. You feel clean and smell clean now. You like that. And you know that inside your body you are starting to get rid of the damaging effects of smoking. You know that in time your body will heal itself because you are no longer going to pump damaging smoke into your body. You feel good about your decision to become a non-smoker and to remain a non-smoker the rest of your life. You look forward to each day of your life as a non-smoker because you will feel better, look better, smell better, and be better than ever before.

I want you to imagine yourself now. See yourself as you really want to be, the real you. Alive and energetic, in full control, serene, and healthy. This is you. This is the real you. This is the person you can really come to be. At this moment you are making yourself a promise . . . a commitment to become the real you. This commitment will be with you, stronger every day. From now on, every day you will become more and more completely the person you want to be. You will be relaxed and calm no matter what is going on around you. And anything that does happen, you can handle it in a relaxed and sensible manner. And you will feel so good, you will have all the energy in the world every single day. And it will be very easy for you to remain a non-smoker every day for the rest of your life. No matter where you are, no matter what you are doing.

In a moment, I am going to count backward from 10 to 1. I want you to count with me silently to yourself. Think each number as I say it, and allow each number to take you deeper. 10 . . . 9 . . . 8 . . . 7 . . . 6 . . . 5 . . . 4 . . . 3 . . . 2 . . . 1. You are now very deeply relaxed. You can give yourself the following suggestions. Say the words to yourself with me as I say them.

I will always be relaxed and calm.

I will not want anything to smoke before, during or after dinner.

Regardless of what happens at work, I will feel relaxed.

I will feel free of the desire to smoke the entire time I am working.

I am in total control of every aspect of my life. Cigarettes no longer have any part in my life.

I am now a non-smoker. I will remain a non-smoker the rest of my life. I have made this healthy decision, and I am happy with that decision. I am in control.

Cigarettes have no control over me any longer. I have resolved to break the bad habit of smoking, and I have broken that bad habit.

Every time you listen to this tape it makes you feel just wonderful. And each time you listen to this tape you will relax completely. You will go just as deep as you are now. Just as you are now, and the suggestions will go deeper and deeper into your mind. By using this tape faithfully every day, you will have perfect control over your desires. You can dissolve away any urge for a cigarette.

You can dissolve away any tension. You can dissolve away any craving for tobacco of any kind, and you will keep on looking better and better, and you will keep on feeling good every single day.

The next time you hear my voice on tape, you will allow yourself to relax even more completely than you are now. And the suggestions I have given you will keep on going deeper and deeper and deeper into your mind.

In a few moments when you awaken yourself, you will feel very very relaxed, and you will be completely refreshed, alive, alert, full of energy, full of confidence. You will feel simply marvelous. All you have to do to awaken is to count with me from one up to five and at the count of five, open your eyes, feeling relaxed, refreshed, alert, in very high spirits. Feeling very good indeed. 1 . . . 2 . . . 3 . . . 4 . . . 5.

• • •

Self-Confidence and Memory Improvement

20

THIS TAPE will enable you to build your self-confidence and to improve your memory. Self-hypnosis can enable you to do anything that you really want to do, but it is not able to force you to do something that you really do not want to do.

You should listen to this tape at least once every day for a week and then once a week after that until you feel that you do not need it any longer. Of course, you may listen to it more often if you wish. The more you listen to it, the stronger and faster the results. If for some reason you are unable to listen every day, be sure to use the tape at least once every week. If you allow more than one week to lapse between sessions, you may not get the results you want because post-hypnotic suggestion weakens in one to two weeks.

Once you have built your self-confidence and memory to where you are satisfied, you need not listen to the tape anymore. However, you may want to listen to it from time to time just for a refresher and reinforcement.

Self-Confidence and
Memory Improvement
Tape Script

Close your eyes and take a deep, full breath and exhale completely, all the way to the bottom of your lungs. All out. Do it again now. Just relax and let it all out. One more time, and this time hold your breath when you have filled your lungs with clean, refreshing, relaxing air. Hold it in. Keep your eyes closed. Now let your breath out slowly and feel yourself relaxing all over.

Focus your attention on your toes now and allow your toes to relax completely. Each toe is loose and heavy. Now let this relaxation flow into your feet, into your ankles, your calves, your knees. Feel it flowing into your thighs, into your hips, into your waist, flowing up into your chest now. Feel your breathing easier and deeper, more regular and more relaxed. Now let the deep relaxed feeling go into your shoulders, down your arms, into your upper arms, your forearms, and into your hands and fingers, and flowing back into your forearms, your upper arms, your shoulders. Flowing into your neck, over your face, your chin, your cheeks, even your ears are relaxed. Feel it flowing into your eyes and eyelids now. Your eyelids are so heavy and smooth. Flowing up into your eyebrows, over your forehead, over the top of your head, down the back of your head, and down the back of your neck.

A new heaviness is starting in your toes now. Twice as heavy as the first time. Imagine a heavy weight on each toe. Feel the heaviness deep and even more relaxed. And this heavy, deep feeling is going into your feet, your ankles, your calves, your knees, going into your thighs, your hips, into your waist. Flowing up into your chest now, relaxing your heart, relaxing your lungs, allowing your breathing to be more intense, more regular, more and more completely relaxed. Now the deep heavy feeling is flowing into your shoulders, and down your arms, your upper arms, your forearms, into your hands and fingers. And now flowing back through your forearms, your upper arms, into your shoulders and into your neck. Flowing over your face, into your eyes, over your eyebrows, over your forehead, over the top of your head, down the back of your head and down the back of your neck.

And a new heaviness is starting now at the top of your head. Twice as heavy as before. Twice as heavy. Imagine a heavy weight on the very top of your head, soft and relaxed and heavy. Feel the heavy relaxation flowing down into your face and eyes now, down through your neck, your shoulders, flowing down through your chest, your waist, your hips, your thighs, your knees, into your calves, your ankles, your feet and toes. Deeply relaxed, loose and limp, and comfortable from the top of your head to the very tip of your toes.

I want you to imagine now that you are looking at a blackboard. On the blackboard imagine a circle. Into the circle we are going to place the letters of the alphabet in reverse order, and with each letter after you place it into the circle, you will erase it then from inside the circle and allow yourself to relax more and more deeply.

Picture the blackboard now. Picture the circle. Into the circle put the letter Z. Now erase the Z from inside the circle, and go deeper. Put Y into the circle, and erase it and go deeper. X, and erase it and go deeper still. W, and erase it. V, and erase it. U, and erase it. T, and erase it. S, and erase it. R, and erase it. Q, and erase it. P, and erase it. O, and erase it. N, and erase it. M, and erase it. L, and erase it. K, and erase it. J, and erase it. I, and erase it. H, and erase it. G, and erase it. F, and erase it. E, and erase it. D, and erase it. C, and erase it. B, and erase it. A, and erase it. Now erase the circle and forget about the blackboard. Just go on relaxing more and more deeply. Feel yourself sink into the chair, mind and body drifting deeper and deeper into relaxation, deeper with each breath.

I want you to imagine now that you are looking at a clear, blue summer sky. And in the sky, a skywriting airplane is writing your first name in fluffy, white cloudlike letters. See your name floating fluffy, white, and cloudlike in a clear, blue sky. Now let your name just dissolve away. Let the winds just blow your name away into the blue. Forget about your name. Forget you even have a name. Names are not important. Just go on listening to my voice and allowing yourself to relax more deeply.

I want you to imagine now that I am placing on each of your knees a heavy bag of sand. Feel the sand pressing down on your knees. Your knees are growing heavier and more relaxed. In the sand is a very powerful numbing ingredient and the numbness is flowing down into your knees now. Your knees are growing numb and more numb under the sand. And the heavy, numb feeling is flowing down into your calves, into your ankles, into your feet and toes. Everything below your knees is numb and more numb from the sand. And now the heavy, numb feeling is going up into your thighs, flowing into your hips, through your waist, and into your chest. It flows into your shoulders, and they grow numb and heavy. It flows down your arms, your upper arms, your forearms, into your hands and fingers. Flowing back now through your forearms, your upper arms, your shoulders, and into your neck. Over your face, your eyes. Flowing up to your eyebrows, your forehead, over the top of your head, down the back of your head, and down the back of your neck.

As you go on floating, drifting smoothly and gently, more and more deeply relaxed with each breath, I want you to focus your attention on the very tip of your nose. Keep your attention focused gently and lazily on the tip of your nose until you reach a point where your entire attention is on the sound of my voice. And when you reach that point, you can forget about your nose and just go on listening to my voice and allowing yourself to relax more and more deeply.

As you keep your attention gently focused on the tip of your nose, I want you to imagine now that you are standing on the stage of a large auditorium filled with people. There are hundreds of people seated in the auditorium and they have all come to hear you speak.

You are delighted to be here because you love sharing your thoughts and ideas with others. You are relaxed and calm as you stand looking out at the audience. You start to speak now, and you notice the audience gives you their undivided attention. They like what you are saying. Someone in the audience asks you a question. Your agile mind quickly and accurately recalls a quotation you have memorized that supplies the answer. You quote so quickly from memory that it seems the ideas expressed are your own. You love interacting with people like this because you feel that you are just as intelligent as anyone else. You realize that you can talk and think just as intelligently as anyone else, and you feel confident in all situations. When you finish speaking, the audience gives you a standing ovation. You feel humble and good because you know you used your innate abilities to contribute to the enjoyment and enrichment of others.

I want you to imagine now that you are studying for an examination. To pass the examination you must correctly give the name of the fifth president of the United States. The correct information is written on a paper in front of you for you to study from. You are relaxed and calm as you study the paper. You feel a tremendous amount of energy with a tremendous concentration power. Your mind is like a soft, absorbent sponge and everything you concentrate on you will absorb like a sponge. When you want to remember what you have concentrated on, you will squeeze your mind like a sponge and you will remember everything you have concentrated on.

Concentrate now on the paper in front of you. It says "fifth president was James Monroe." See the number five and the name James Monroe. Whenever you wish to recall this in the future just cast your eyes upward and ask yourself who the fifth president of the United States was. Immediately you will see or recall the number five and the name James Monroe. Do this now. Keeping your eyes closed, just cast them upward and ask who the fifth president was. Imagine that you see the number five and the name James Monroe.

Now you throw the paper away. You take out a blank sheet of paper and write on it "the fifth president of the United States was James Monroe." You have passed the test perfectly and you have learned how to concentrate and to remember anything that you have concentrated on.

I want you to imagine yourself now. See yourself as you really want to be, the real you. Alive and energetic, in full control, calm and confident with an excellent memory. This is you. This is the real you. This is the person you can really come to be. At this moment you are making yourself a promise . . . a commitment to become the real you. This commitment will be with you, stronger every day. From now on, every day you will become more and more completely the person you want to be. You will be relaxed and calm no matter what is going on around you. And anything that does happen, you can handle it in a relaxed and sensible manner. And you will feel so good, you will have all the energy in the world every single day. And it will be very easy for you to achieve the success and happiness you want and deserve. For you are a product of your own thought patterns. Think success, and you are a success. Think confidently and you become a confident person. Think beauty and you become a beautiful person. Think strength and you become strong. Think positively and constructively, and your life becomes a positive and constructive experience. These things are your new image . . . the new you . . . stronger and stronger every day.

You are now learning to be in total control of every aspect of your life. You will always be relaxed and calm and in control. No longer will you allow others to exercise control over you. Never again will you be a slave to anything, to any person, or to any job. You are your own person, and you are in control.

In a moment, I am going to count backward from 10 to 1. I want you to count with me silently to yourself. Think each number as I say it, and allow each number to take you deeper.

10 . . . 9 . . . 8 . . . 7 . . . 6 . . . 5 . . . 4 . . . 3 . . . 2 . . . 1.

You are now very deeply relaxed. You can give yourself the following suggestions. Say the words to yourself with me as I say them.

I will always be relaxed and calm no matter what is happening. And anything that does happen, I can handle it in a sensible and mature manner.

I think of the present and future only.

I have an excellent mind and memory, and I use them more and more effectively every day.

I have a tremendous and intense concentration power with everything I do, and I remember more effectively everything I concentrate on.

I can trigger my memory recall by simply casting my eyes upward about forty-five degrees and mentally asking for the information I wish to recall.

I feel the energy, drive, and desire to go out socially, and I will go out socially.

I feel positive that everything in my life will work out for me, and I feel good about myself and the direction my life is now going in.

Every time you listen to this tape it makes you feel just wonderful. And each time you listen to this tape you will relax completely. You will go just as deep as you are now. Just as you are now, and the suggestions will go deeper and deeper into your mind. By using this tape faithfully every day, you will have perfect control over your life. You can dissolve away any fear. You can dissolve away any tension. You can dissolve away any shyness or feelings of inadequacy. You will keep on performing better and better, and you will keep on feeling good every single day. You are an intelligent and worthwhile person. And every day from now on you will become more completely the person you really want to be. You will be confident, relaxed, poised, charming, optimistic, and firm in your resolution to do what you want for your own happiness.

Your mind is always focused, alert, and clear. You can memorize anything you wish quickly and easily, and you can recall anything in your mind quickly and easily.

You have complete faith in yourself to properly handle any situation you encounter because you have taken complete control of your own life in every respect.

Repeat the following suggestion to yourself three times as I say it:

"I am a confident and successful person and I am in total control of my life."

"I am a confident and successful person and I am in total control of my life."

"I am a confident and successful person and I am in total control of my life."

You will never allow yourself to be intimidated by any person, organization, or situation because you are now in control. You have total confidence in your own ability to make all decisions that affect your life.

The next time you hear my voice on tape, you will allow yourself to relax even more completely than you are now. And the suggestions I have given you will keep on going deeper and deeper and deeper into your mind.

In a few moments when you awaken yourself, you will feel very very relaxed, and you will be completely refreshed, alive, alert, full of energy, full of confidence. You will feel simply marvelous. All you have to do to awaken is to count with me from one up to five and at the count of five, open your eyes, feeling relaxed, refreshed, alert, in very high spirits. Feeling very good indeed. 1 . . . 2 . . . 3 . . . 4 . . . 5.

●　　●　　●

Maintaining Good Health

21

THIS TAPE is intended to help you expand your health maintenance program by enlisting the aid of your own creative ability and self-healing ability under the power of self-hypnosis. Many people have been helped by hypnosis, and you may be also.

This tape will take you into an altered state of consciousness that will help you to maintain good health by creating and reinforcing the image of yourself in good health, as you really want to be, and then taking the steps to make that image become reality in the physical world.

At a minimum, I recommend that you use this tape at least once every other week to help you maintain good health, free of illness, pain, or lack of energy. It would be even better if you use this tape every week, or even more often. This tape is not a one-time thing. It is designed to give you a tool to use for the rest of your life to aid you in maintaining good health.

If you should become ill or injured, you should use the tape script Self-Healing from the next chapter to aid you in healing yourself. Of course, you should also follow the guidance of your medical practitioner. This tape is not a substitute for competent medical help.

Maintaining Good Health
Tape Script

Close your eyes and take a deep, full breath and exhale completely, all the way to the bottom of your lungs. All out. Do it again now. Just relax and let it all out. One more time, and this time hold your breath when you have filled your lungs with clean, refreshing, relaxing air. Hold it in. Keep your eyes closed. Now let your breath out slowly and feel yourself relaxing all over.

I want you to imagine now that all your tensions, all your tightness, and all your fears and worries are draining away from the top of your head. Let it drain down through your face, down through your neck, through your shoulders, through your chest, your waist, your hips, your thighs, down through your knees, your calves, your ankles, your feet, and out your toes. All your tension, all your tightness, all your worries and fears are draining away now from the very tips of your toes, and you are relaxing more and more.

Focus your attention on your toes now and allow your toes to relax completely. Each toe is loose and heavy. Now let this relaxation flow into your feet, into your ankles, your calves, your knees. Feel it flowing into your thighs, into your hips, into your waist, flowing up into your chest now. Feel your breathing easier and deeper, more regular and more relaxed. Now let the deep relaxed feeling go into your shoulders, down your arms, into your upper arms, your forearms, and into your hands and fingers, and flowing back into your forearms, your upper arms, your shoulders. Flowing into your neck, over your face, your chin, your cheeks, even your ears are relaxed. Feel it flowing into your eyes and eyelids now. Your eyelids are so heavy and smooth. Flowing up into your eyebrows, over your forehead, over the top of your head, down the back of your head, and down the back of your neck.

And a new heaviness is starting now at the top of your head. Twice as heavy as before. Twice as heavy. Imagine a heavy weight on the very top of your head, soft and relaxed and heavy. Feel the heavy relaxation flowing down into your face and eyes now, down through your neck, your shoulders, flowing down through your chest, your waist, your hips, your thighs, your knees, into your calves, your ankles, your feet and toes. Deeply relaxed, loose and limp, and comfortable from the top of your head to the very tip of your toes.

I want you to imagine now that you are looking at a blackboard. On the blackboard imagine a circle. Into the circle we are going to place the letters of the alphabet in reverse order, and with each letter after you place it into the circle, you will erase it then from inside the circle and allow yourself to relax more and more deeply.

Picture the blackboard now. Picture the circle. Into the circle put the letter Z. Now erase the Z from inside the circle, and go deeper. Put Y into the circle, and erase it and go deeper. X, and erase it and go deeper still. W, and erase it. V, and erase it. U, and erase it. T, and erase it. S, and erase it. R, and erase it. Q, and erase it. P, and erase it. O, and erase it. N, and erase it. M, and erase it. L, and erase it. K, and erase it. J, and erase it. I, and erase it. H, and erase it. G, and erase it. F, and erase it. E, and erase it. D, and erase it. C, and erase it. B, and erase it. A, and erase it. Now erase the circle and forget about the blackboard. Just go on relaxing more and more deeply. Feel yourself sink into the chair, mind and body drifting deeper and deeper into relaxation, deeper with each breath.

As you breathe in, imagine that you are breathing in a pure, clean, odorless anesthesia. The anesthesia is flowing all throughout your body now. It is a warm, numb, tingling feeling, and the more you breathe in, the more you want to breathe in, and you allow your breathing to become even deeper now, bringing in more and more of this peaceful, relaxing, tranquil feeling. From now on until the end of this session, you will allow yourself to relax more and more completely with each breath you take.

I want you to imagine now that you are standing on the top step of a heavy wooden staircase. Feel the carpet under your feet. The carpet can be any kind and color you wish . . . create it. Now extend your hand out and touch the railing. Feel the smooth polished wood of the railing under your hand. You are standing just ten steps up from the floor below. The stairs are curving very smoothly down to the floor below. In a moment we will walk down the stairs. With each step down you will allow yourself to relax even more deeply. By the time you reach the floor below you will be deeper than you have ever gone before. Take a step down now, down to the ninth step smoothly and easily. Feel yourself going deeper. Now down to eight, deeper still. Now down to seven . . . six . . . five . . . four . . . three. . . two . . . one. Now you are standing on the floor below. There are two doors in front of you. One door has the number one on it, and a sign that says HEALTH. The other door has the number two on it, and a sign that says HEALING. Reach out now and open door number one, the health door. A flood of light comes streaming out through the open door. Walk into the room, into the light through the open door. You are inside the room now, look around you. This is your room, your very own private inner place and you are free here. Free to create, free to be who you are. Free to do whatever you will, and the light that shines in this room is your light. Feel the light all around you, shining on you; feel the energy in the light. Let the light flow all through your body now. Going in through every pore in your skin. Filling you completely. Pushing away all doubt. Pushing out all fear and tension. Pushing out all harmful substances from your body. Pushing out all negative thoughts. You are filled with the light. You are clear and radiant, glowing with the shining light in your room.

In this room you have the ability to reinforce thoughts, words, and actions that contribute to your health. What you do in this room will help you to remain healthy, and this is so, because this is your special inner place where you are in total control of your destiny.

In this room you will establish the rules and patterns you need for good health. Then you will resolve to make the rules and patterns a living part of your daily life. When you do this, you will continue to remain healthy.

Take a few moments now to put some beneficial things in your room. A shower, so you can keep your body clean. An exercise bicycle so you can perform physical exercise. Some books on nutrition. A bottle of multivitamin tablets. A comfortable chair to rest in and meditate. I will stop talking now for 20 seconds while you put these things and anything else you wish in your room.

PAUSE 20 SECONDS

Now repeat the following five health statements to yourself with me as I say them.

1. Cleanliness is important to my good health.
2. Physical exercise is important to my good health.
3. A nutritious diet is important to my good health.
4. Accident and disease prevention are important to my good health.
5. A positive attitude is important to my good health.

Now walk over to your shower and take your clothes off. In a few moments you will take a refreshing shower to rid your body of all contamination. At this level of the mind, one second is equivalent to two minutes of actual time. I will stop talking now for five seconds while you take a 10 minute shower. Begin now to take your shower.

PAUSE 5 SECONDS

Now dry your body and put your clothes back on.

PAUSE 3 SECONDS

Make the following commitment to yourself as I say it: "I shall keep my body clean and free from contaminants by taking baths or showers daily. I shall also wash my hands periodically throughout the day because I know my hands are the most likely part of my body to come in contact with contaminants."

You have now committed yourself to keeping yourself clean. This is the first important step to maintaining good health. Do not become obsessed or fanatical about cleanliness. Just use common sense. A wise guideline is "All things in moderation."

Take a deep breath and relax even more.

Now walk over to your exercise bicycle and get on it. In a few moments you will get some beneficial exercise by taking a 20-minute ride. At this level of the mind one second is equivalent to two minutes of actual time. I will stop talking now for 10 seconds while you take a 20-minute ride. Begin now to ride your exercise bicycle.

PAUSE 10 SECONDS

You may stop riding now and get off the bicycle. Take a towel and dry the perspiration on your face.

PAUSE 3 SECONDS

Make the following commitment to yourself as I say it: "I shall find a way to perform some exercise each week in order to keep my body physically fit."

You have now committed yourself to keeping yourself physically fit through regular exercise. This is the second important step to maintaining good health. Do not become obsessed or fanatical about physical exercise. Just use common sense. A brisk walk is excellent exercise. A wise guideline is "All things in moderation."

Take a deep breath and relax even more.

There is a table in your room that has some nutritious food on it. Walk over to the table and observe the food. Fresh fruits. Fresh vegetables. Fresh fish. Grains. And much more. Add any special nutritious foods you like. Take a few moments now to observe the delicious food.

PAUSE 5 SECONDS

Make the following commitment to yourself as I say it: "I shall strive to eat a balanced nutritious diet every day."

You have now committed yourself to keep yourself healthy by eating a nutritious, balanced diet. This is the third important step to maintaining good health. Do not become obsessed or fanatical about your diet. Just use common sense. Read a book on nutrition. A wise guideline is "All things in moderation."

Take a deep breath and relax even more.

The table in your room now contains several items that relate to accident and disease prevention. Walk over to the table. There is an automobile seat belt on the table. Pick it up and examine it.

PAUSE 5 SECONDS

Seat belts can save your life or prevent serious injury. Make the following commitment to yourself as I say it: "I shall always wear a seat belt when in a vehicle, and I shall always use safety devices and protective clothing whenever I am engaged in potentially dangerous activities."

There is a condom on the table. Pick it up and examine it.

PAUSE 5 SECONDS

A condom will protect you from the deadly AIDS virus, from syphilis and gonorrhea and other sexually transmitted diseases. Make the following commitment to yourself as I say it: "I shall always insist on the use of condoms to help protect me from sexually transmitted diseases."

There are hundreds of ways to injure yourself or to allow yourself to become ill. But all the ways require you to be careless or to not use common sense. Accident and illness prevention is the fourth important step to having a healthy life. This is the one step you must be obsessed with and you must be fanatical about your physical protection at all times. So make this commitment to yourself as I say it: "I shall use common sense and shall be constantly alert to protect myself from disease and injury."

Take a deep breath and relax even more.

Now walk over to your chair and sit in it. It is time for you to meditate on the fifth important step to maintaining good health. This may be the most important step of all because it pertains to your mental health. You are what you think you are. By making a positive attitude part of your daily life, you create a positive life for yourself. This means good health.

I want you to meditate now on the blessings and good things in your life. I will stop talking for one minute while you meditate. Begin now.

PAUSE 60 SECONDS

Now make the following commitment to yourself as I say it: "I shall direct my thoughts every day to the good, positive aspects of my life."

Now I will stop talking for one minute while you meditate on the names and faces of those people you wish to send love to. Begin now.

PAUSE 60 SECONDS

Now make the following commitment to yourself as I say it, "I shall strive every day to be more loving and to express my love and friendship."

For your final meditation I will stop talking for one minute while you meditate in a positive manner on any aspect of your life that you wish. Begin now.

PAUSE 60 SECONDS

Now make the following commitment to yourself as I say it: "I shall become the very best I can be by maintaining a positive mental attitude about myself and about life in general."

Take a deep breath and relax even more.

You have just reviewed the five important steps to maintaining your good health and you have committed to yourself to follow these steps: cleanliness, physical exercise, nutritious diet, disease and accident prevention, and a positive mental attitude.

While you are standing in the light in your room, I want you to build an image. An image of yourself as you really want to be. Not as someone else wants you to be, but as you really want yourself to be. See your image standing in front of you in the light. See the quiet look of confidence on the face of your image.

Notice the healthy body. Notice how calm and free your image is. I will stop talking now for sixty seconds while you give your image all the qualities and attributes you wish it to have.

PAUSE 60 SECONDS

Now take a final look at your image. This is you. This is the real you. This is the person you are now becoming. Walk closer to your image now. Walk closer. Now walk into your image. Let it blend into your very body. Your own best self, a living part of you now. Stronger every day.

From now on every day you will be more and more completely the healthy person you really want to be. You will be relaxed and calm. And no matter what is going on around you, you can handle it in a relaxed and sensible manner. And you will feel so good. You will have all the energy you can use every single day. And it will be so easy for you to stay in complete control of every aspect of your life. You will find it very easy to dispel all fears, anxieties, doubts, and troubles. You are in total control of your life, and this is so.

Now take one final look around your room. What you do in your room has no limit. No limit.

You have just experienced using the altered state of consciousness to go deep within yourself to a private, powerful, creative place that you can use to help you maintain good health. You have been given this valuable tool to use to enrich your life. Use it to help you create and maintain good health. The choice is yours alone to do or not to do. For you are in control now. And whatever you choose to do, you can do. Whatever you set your own mind to achieve, you can and will achieve it. You will be completely successful and you will enjoy your success. And you will enjoy being healthy and energetic every day.

The next time you hear my voice on tape, you will allow yourself to relax ten times more deeply relaxed than you are now. And the suggestions I give you then will go ten times deeper into your mind.

In a few moments when you awaken yourself, you will feel very, very relaxed and you will feel completely refreshed, alive, alert, full of energy and full of self-confidence. You will feel simply marvelous. All you have to do to awaken yourself is to count with me from one up to five and at the count of five you will awaken feeling relaxed, refreshed, alert, and in very high spirits. Feeling very good indeed. 1 . . . 2 . . . 3 . . . 4 . . . 5. Open eyes, wide awake and feeling fine, feeling better than before, and this is so!

● ● ●

Self-Healing

22

THIS TAPE is intended to help you heal illness or injury by enlisting the aid of your own creative ability and self-healing ability under the power of self-hypnosis.

This tape will direct you into an altered state of consciousness that will help you to deal with illness or injury by using your creative mind to destroy harmful intrusions in your body. You will direct your body to heal quickly and effectively. Of course, you should also be following the advice of your medical practitioner.

At a minimum, you should use this tape at least once every day until you are healed of the illness or injury. It would be even better if you used this tape several times a day until your health is restored. This tape is a tool you can use for the rest of your life if illness or injury should befall you.

Once your health is restored, you should use the Maintaining Good Health tape (Chapter 22) to help you to maintain your health. If you use the Maintaining Good Health tape regularly, you should be able to minimize, or perhaps totally eliminate, illness. Of course, you should also follow the guidance of your medical practitioner. This tape is not a substitute for competent medical help.

Self-Healing
Tape Script

Close your eyes and take a deep, full breath and exhale completely, all the way to the bottom of your lungs. All out. Do it again now. Just relax and let it all out. One more time, and this time hold your breath when you have filled your lungs with clean, refreshing, relaxing air. Hold it in. Keep your eyes closed. Now let your breath out slowly and feel yourself relaxing all over.

I want you to imagine now that all your tensions, all your tightness, and all your fears and worries are draining away from the top of your head. Let it drain down through your face, down through your neck, through your shoulders, through your chest, your waist, your hips, your thighs, down through your knees, your calves, your ankles, your feet and out your toes. All your tension, all your tightness, all your worries and fears are draining away now from the very tips of your toes, and you are relaxing more and more.

Focus your attention on your toes now and allow your toes to relax completely. Each toe is loose and heavy. Now let this relaxation flow into your feet, into your ankles, your calves, your knees. Feel it flowing into your thighs, into your hips, into your waist, flowing up into your chest now. Feel your breathing easier and deeper, more regular and more relaxed. Now let the deep relaxed feeling go into your shoulders, down your arms, into your upper arms, your forearms, and into your hands and fingers, and flowing back into your forearms, your upper arms, your shoulders. Flowing into your neck, over your face, your chin, your cheeks, even your ears are relaxed. Feel it flowing into your eyes and eyelids now. Your eyelids are so heavy and smooth. Flowing up into your eyebrows, over your forehead, over the top of your head, down the back of your head, and down the back of your neck.

And a new heaviness is starting now at the top of your head. Twice as heavy as before. Twice as heavy. Imagine a heavy weight on the very top of your head, soft and relaxed and heavy. Feel the heavy relaxation flowing down into your face and eyes now, down through your neck, your shoulders, flowing down through your chest, your waist, your hips, your thighs, your knees, into your calves, your ankles, your feet and toes. Deeply relaxed, loose and limp, and comfortable from the top of your head to the very tip of your toes.

I want you to imagine now that you are looking at a blackboard. On the blackboard imagine a circle. Into the circle we are going to place the letters of the alphabet in reverse order, and with each letter after you place it into the circle, you will erase it then from inside the circle and allow yourself to relax more and more deeply.

Picture the blackboard now. Picture the circle. Into the circle put the letter Z. Now erase the Z from inside the circle, and go deeper. Put Y into the circle, and erase it and go deeper. X, and erase it and go deeper still. W, and erase it. V, and erase it. U, and erase it. T, and erase it. S, and erase it. R, and erase it. Q, and erase it. P, and erase it. O, and erase it. N, and erase it. M, and erase it. L, and erase it. K, and erase it. J, and erase it. I, and erase it. H, and erase it. G, and erase it. F, and erase it. E, and erase it. D, and erase it. C, and erase it. B, and erase it. A, and erase it. Now erase the circle and forget about the blackboard. Just go on relaxing more and more deeply. Feel yourself sink into the chair, mind and body drifting deeper and deeper into relaxation, deeper with each breath.

As you breathe in, imagine that you are breathing in a pure, clean, odorless anesthesia. The anesthesia is flowing all throughout your body now. It is a warm, numb, tingling feeling, and the more you breathe in, the more you want to breathe in, and you allow your breathing to become even deeper now, bringing in more and more of this peaceful, relaxing, tranquil feeling. From now on until the end of this session, you will allow yourself to relax more and more completely with each breath you take.

I want you to imagine now that you are standing on the top step of a heavy wooden staircase. Feel the carpet under your feet. The carpet can be any kind and color you wish . . . create it. Now extend your hand out and touch the railing. Feel the smooth polished wood of the railing under your hand. You are standing just ten steps up from the floor below. The stairs are curving very smoothly down to the floor below. In a moment we will walk down the stairs. With each step down you will allow yourself to relax even more deeply. By the time you reach the floor below you will be deeper than you have ever gone before. Take a step down now, down to the ninth step smoothly and easily. Feel yourself going deeper. Now down to eight, deeper still. Now down to seven . . . six . . . five . . . four . . . three . . . two . . . one. Now you are standing on the floor below. There are two doors in front of you. One door has the number one on it, and a sign that says HEALTH. The other door has the number two on it, and a sign that says HEALING. Reach out now and open door number two, the healing door. A flood of light comes streaming out through the open doorway. Walk into the room, into the light through the open door. You are inside the room now, look around you. This is your room, your very own private inner healing place and you are free here. Free to create, free to be who you are. Free to do whatever you will, and the light that shines in this room is your healing light. Feel the healing light all around you, shining on you; feel the healing energy in the light. Let the healing light flow all through your body now. Going in through every pore in your skin. Filling you completely. Pushing away all doubt.

Pushing out all fear and tension. Pushing out all harmful germs, viruses, infections, poisons, bacteria, and other harmful substances from your body. You are filled with the light. You are clear and radiant, glowing with the shining light in your room.

In this room you have the ability to reinforce thoughts, words, and actions that contribute to you becoming healed. What you do in this room will help you to heal yourself, and this is so, because this is your special inner place where you are in total control of your destiny.

Here in your healing room you have some special things to help you overcome illness and injury. In the center of the room is a soft, comfortable blue chair that can recline and swivel. It is blue because blue is a healing color. Observe your chair.

PAUSE 3 SECONDS

Go over to your chair and sit in it.

PAUSE 3 SECONDS

Feel how comfortable it is. Feel the healing blue color caress and penetrate your body. In this chair you will be able to rest, meditate, and heal yourself.

Now look directly in front of you. There is a full-length mirror just two feet in front of you. It has a gold frame around it. Observe your mirror.

PAUSE 3 SECONDS

Your mirror is a healing mirror that has some special features that you will use shortly.

To your left, within arm's reach, is a large blue box with wires and two plastic tubes connected to it. This is your special instrument that you will use shortly to purify your blood. Observe it.

PAUSE 3 SECONDS

To your right, within arm's reach, is a blue cosmic medicine cabinet that contains anything you need to restore your body to health. You will use it shortly. Observe it.

PAUSE 3 SECONDS

Your medicine cabinet also has a water dispenser and paper drinking cups, which you will use shortly. Observe it.

PAUSE 3 SECONDS

In a few moments you will begin to perform some extraordinary healing on yourself. At no time will you have any pain. At no time will you feel ill. In fact, you will feel just fine throughout the entire healing procedure, and this is so.

Now you are ready to begin your self-healing. The first important step is to adjust your mental attitude so you have no harmful, hateful, negative energies. Follow my instructions now on how to adjust your attitude for better mental health.

Take a deep breath, and relax even more, going to a deeper level of mind.

Repeat the following two statements to yourself with me as I say them.

"I forgive myself for all of my thoughts, words and actions that were negative toward others or myself."

"I forgive all others for their thoughts, words and actions that were negative and directed toward me."

I will now stop talking for 30 seconds while you send love to those people who are special to you.

PAUSE 30 SECONDS

Your attitude and mental health are now more positively adjusted. Repeat the following suggestion to yourself as I say it: "Every day in every way I am getting better and better."

Turn your chair to your right now so you are facing your cosmic medicine cabinet. On it sits three bottles. One is labeled HEALING LOTION. The second is labeled VITAMINS.

The third is labeled CURE-ALL. In a few moments you will have the opportunity to use these, but first let me tell you about these cosmic medicines.

The healing lotion is used to heal any injury or disease on your body. If you have such an injury or disease, all you need to do is take the lotion and apply it to that part of your body that you desire to be healed. As you apply it, think to yourself, "I am being healed."

The vitamins are cosmic capsules that contain all the vitamins and minerals in the proper dosage that you currently need for your body.

The cure-all bottle contains pills for aiding in the cure of every illness or infection there is. All you need to do is swallow one pill while saying to yourself, "I am now being cured of . . . " and then mentally state what illness it is you have. If you don't know the name of your illness, just make a generic statement such as "I am now being cured of my stomach problems" or "I am now being cured of whatever is afflicting me." You get the idea.

Let us begin.

First, reach out and get your vitamin bottle and a cup of water. I will stop talking now for ten seconds while you swallow your vitamin capsule. Do it now.

PAUSE 10 SECONDS

Good. You have now enriched your body with vitamins and minerals you need.

In a few moments I will stop talking for 30 seconds while you use your lotion or take your cure-all pills for your specific illness or injury. You know what is currently wrong, and now is your chance to begin fixing it. Be sure to mentally reaffirm that you are being healed while you use the cure-all pills or lotion. You may begin now.

PAUSE 30 SECONDS

Very good. Now you are ready to purify your blood. Swivel your chair to the left so you can face your purification box.

PAUSE 3 SECONDS

Reach out and get the two plastic tubes. Connect one tube to anywhere on the left side of your body. On your arm, leg, side. Wherever you wish.

PAUSE 3 SECONDS

Connect the other tube to anywhere on the right side of your body.

PAUSE 3 SECONDS

Now turn on your machine by pressing the ON button.

Notice now how the tubes have filled up with your blood. There is no pain. You feel fine.

Your machine is taking blood from your right side and purifying it and then putting the purified blood back into your body on the left side. This entire procedure will take 10 seconds. I will stop talking while you purify your blood.

PAUSE 10 SECONDS

Your blood is now purified. Before you disconnect the machine, there is one other thing you need to do. This machine has the power to put tiny sharks into your blood stream. These are very beneficial, friendly sharks. These sharks eat only harmful germs, viruses, bacteria, infection, and cancer cells. In a few moments when your friendly sharks enter your blood stream, you can mentally tell them any specific things you want them to destroy. For example, you can tell them to destroy cancer cells, or AIDS virus, or tuberculosis, or infection. You know what you want eliminated from your body, so tell the sharks when they enter your blood.

Now reach out and press the red button on your machine. This will release the friendly sharks. I will stop talking for 10 seconds while the sharks swim into your blood and you tell them what to destroy. Do it now.

PAUSE 10 SECONDS

You may now turn off your machine by pressing the OFF button and then disconnect the plastic tubes from your body. Your blood is now filled with your sharks, which will seek out and destroy whatever you told them to.

PAUSE 3 SECONDS

Now you are ready for the most dramatic and powerful of all your self-healing techniques. Swivel around to face your full-length, gold framed healing mirror.

See yourself in the mirror. This powerful mirror gives you the ability to completely repair your body. I will explain how it works, and then I will give you 90 seconds to do it.

Just by wishing to do so, you can examine any part of your body, inside and out, in your healing mirror. If there is anything you wish to repair or replace, you can do so. Let me give you a couple examples. Suppose your heart seems defective to you—perhaps the color isn't healthy or it isn't pumping blood like you think it should. Replace it. Your cosmic medicine cabinet has any healthy body part you need. Just unplug the defective heart from your mirror image and then plug in a healthy replacement that you get from your cosmic medicine cabinet. You can do this with any body parts. Suppose your nerves are broken or frayed. Replace them with good ones.

You can also repair things. You see a tear in your skin—sew it up. There are tools for everything in your cosmic medicine cabinet. Perhaps you see a growth or scales on a part of your body. Scrape it off, cut it off, grind or burn it off, whatever you choose.

At this level of the mind, and using your cosmic healing mirror, you can visualize and repair your entire body. In a few moments I will stop talking for 90 seconds while you scan your entire body inside and out and fix anything that needs it. Do not be concerned about time. If you don't get finished, you can come back here again later and continue your work until you have restored your health. Begin now.

PAUSE 90 SECONDS

Excellent. You have now completed a self-healing procedure to restore your body to the health you want.

Look at your image in your mirror now. See how much better it is.

Now walk into your image in your mirror. Let the image blend into your body, a living part of you now healthier every day.

Look above you now. The Sun is directly overhead. It is warm, and its rays are healing rays.

Allow the Sun to come down until it rests on your head.

PAUSE 5 SECONDS

Now allow the Sun to enter your head and gently move down through your body. Warming you. Healing you.

Down through your chest, your waist, your legs, and into your toes.

The Sun moves back up now through your legs, hips, waist, chest, neck, head and out the top of your head to return high above you.

From now on, every day you will be more and more completely the healthy person you really want to be. You will be relaxed and calm. And no matter what is going on around you, you can handle it in a relaxed and sensible manner. And you will feel so good. You will have all the energy you can use every single day. And it will be so easy for you to stay in complete control of every aspect of your life. You will find it very easy to dispel all fears, anxieties, doubts, and troubles. You are in total control of your life, and this is so.

Now take one final look around your room. You can come back here anytime you wish. What you do in your room has no limit. No limit.

You have just experienced using the altered state of consciousness to go deep within yourself to a private, powerful, creative place that you can use to help you heal yourself from illness or injury. You have been given this valuable tool to use to help you get well. Use it to help yourself heal faster and more effectively. The choice is yours alone to do or not to do. For you are in control now. And whatever you choose to do, you can do. Whatever you set your own mind to achieve, you can and will achieve it. You will be completely successful and you will enjoy your success. And you will enjoy feeling better and being better every day.

The next time you hear my voice on tape, you will allow yourself to relax ten times more deeply relaxed than you are now. And the suggestions I give you then will go ten times deeper into your mind.

In a few moments when you awaken yourself, you will feel very relaxed and you will feel completely refreshed, alive, alert, full of energy and full of self-confidence. You will feel much better than before because you know your body is healing itself better than before.

All you have to do to awaken yourself is to count with me from one up to five and at the count of five you will awaken feeling relaxed, refreshed, alert, and in very high spirits. Feeling much better than before. 1 . . . 2 . . . 3 . . . 4 . . . 5. Open eyes, wide awake and feeling better than before, and this is so!

● ● ●

World Peace
(Tape One)

THIS TAPE will help you to remove the power of war from your consciousness and from mass consciousness while also helping to increase the power of peace in your consciousness and in mass consciousness.

This self-hypnosis procedure will guide you into an altered state where you will actually bridge your consciousness into the psychic realm where you will be more effective in projecting your thoughts and energies.

World Peace
Tape Script One

Close your eyes.

Take a deep breath and slowly exhale as you begin to relax.

In a moment I will count slowly from ten down to one. I want you to visualize each number as I say it and allow each number to take you into a deeper state of relaxation.

Ten. Visualize the number ten and relax.

Nine. See a nine, and go deeper.

Eight. See eight, and go deeper still.

Seven. Visualize a seven and relax even more.

Six. See a six. Deeper and Deeper.

Five. See five. Deeper still.

Four. See four. Relax more.

Three. Visualize the number three. Go deeper. More relaxed.

Two. See a two. You are very relaxed.

One. See the number one. You are very relaxed and you will continue to drift deeper with every breath you exhale, and this is so.

I want you to imagine now that you are looking at a clear, blue summer sky. In the sky, a skywriting airplane is writing your first name in white, fluffy cloudlike letters. See your first name in the sky, white, fluffy, cloudlike.

PAUSE 3 SECONDS

Now let your name just drift away. Let the wind just blow your name away into the blue. Forget about your name. Forget you even have a name. Names are not important. Just go on listening to my voice as you relax and go deeper with every breath you exhale.

I want you to imagine now that you are looking into a mirror the size of a movie screen. This mirror is divided into four sections, an upper left, an upper right, a lower left, and a lower right. The mirror has a black frame around it. At the top of the mirror is a sign that says WAR. See the black framed mirror with the label WAR.

PAUSE 5 SECONDS

In a moment you will see reflections in this mirror of some of the things associated with war.

PAUSE 3 SECONDS

Look into the upper left section of the mirror and see the reflection that is now forming there. Visualize a group of men, women and children in the mirror. See them. Imagine them. Now visualize soldiers with machine guns pointing their guns at the group of men, women and children. See the soldiers fire their guns. See the men, women and children fall down dead. This section of the war mirror is called "Destroyer of Innocent Lives."

Now mentally repeat this phrase with me as I say it: "I do not want war to ever occur again. I say NO to war!"

Now take a red crayon and write the word NO in bold letters across this reflection in the mirror.

PAUSE 5 SECONDS

Now I want you to say out loud this same phrase with me as I say it again. "I do not want war to ever occur again. I say NO to war!"

PAUSE 3 SECONDS

Now look into the upper right section of the mirror and see the reflection that is now forming there. Visualize a group of young women holding babies in their arms in this section of the mirror. See them.

Imagine them. These are young mothers and wives who will never again see their husbands who have been killed in war. The babies will never see their fathers. This section of the war mirror is called "The Widow Maker."

Now mentally repeat this phrase with me as I say it: "I do not want war to ever occur again. I say NO to war!"

Now take your red crayon and write the word NO in bold letters across this reflection in the mirror.

PAUSE 5 SECONDS

Now I want you to say out loud this same phrase with me as I say it again. "I do not want war to ever occur again. I say NO to war!"

PAUSE 3 SECONDS

Now look into the lower left section of the mirror and see the reflection that is now forming there. Visualize a large globe of the world sitting on a stand. A group of men have their arms around the globe and are trying to take it away from the other men. See them. Imagine them. These are the leaders of nations who are trying to control the world and deprive others of having any control. This section of the war mirror is called "Lust for Power."

Now mentally repeat this phrase with me as I say it. "I do not want war to ever occur again. I say NO to war!"

Now take your red crayon and write the word NO in bold letters across this reflection in the mirror.

PAUSE 5 SECONDS

Now I want you to say out loud this same phrase with me as I say it again. "I do not want war to ever occur again. I say NO to war!"

PAUSE 3 SECONDS

Now look into the lower right section of the mirror and see the reflection that is now forming there. Visualize a group of merchants. They are selling guns, aircraft, explosives, knives, ammunition, and other weapons of war. Other men are taking these weapons and are giving the merchants large stacks of money in return for them. See them. Imagine them. This section of the mirror is called "Greed."

Now mentally repeat this phrase with me as I say it. "I do not want war to ever occur again. I say NO to war!"

Now take the red crayon and write the word NO in bold letters across this reflection in the mirror.

PAUSE 5 SECONDS

Now I want you to say out loud this same phrase with me as I say it again. "I do not want war to ever occur again. I say NO to war!"

PAUSE 3 SECONDS

You have now examined four of the many ugly aspects of war. War is the "Destroyer Of Innocent Lives. War is a "Widow Maker." War is born in the "Lust For Power." War is promoted by "Greed."

Take one final look at the four reflections in the war mirror. You don't like what you see.

PAUSE 3 SECONDS

If you are right-handed, look down by your right foot. There is a golden brick by your right foot. If you are left-handed, look down by your left foot. There is a golden brick by your left foot.

PAUSE 3 SECONDS

Pick up the golden brick and throw it as hard as you can into the black framed mirror of war, smashing the mirror into tiny pieces.

PAUSE 5 SECONDS

The mirror of war no longer exists.

PAUSE 3 SECONDS

You have destroyed war in your consciousness, and this is so.

PAUSE 3 SECONDS

I want you to imagine now that you are looking into a different mirror the size of a movie screen. This mirror is divided into four sections—an upper left, an upper right, a lower left, and a lower right. This mirror is unbreakable and it has a gold frame around it. At the top of the mirror is a sign that says PEACE. See the gold framed mirror with the label PEACE.

PAUSE 5 SECONDS

In a moment you will see reflections in this mirror of some of the things associated with Peace.

PAUSE 5 SECONDS

Look into the upper left section of the mirror and see the reflection that is now forming there. Visualize a busy city street. On a tall building, visualize the flag of your country waving proudly in the breeze. See a white dove with an olive branch in its mouth fly to the flag-pole and sit on top of it. Down at street level see men, women, and children crowding the sidewalks. The people are smiling. Some stop to shake hands with another person. Others meet friends and they hug each other. A policeman is directing traffic in the street, and he does not have a gun. There are people of all races. Asian. African. Caucasian. Brown. Red. Mulatto. All races. See this scene. Imagine it. Feel the warmth of friendliness. These are people of the world living in peace and harmony. This section of the peace mirror is called "Freedom from Fear."

Now mentally repeat this phrase with me as I say it: "I love peace, and I want peace for everyone, forever. I say YES to peace!"

Now take a green crayon and write the word YES in bold letters across this reflection in the mirror.

PAUSE 5 SECONDS

Now I want you to say out loud this same phrase with me as I say it again. "I love peace, and I want peace for everyone, forever. I say YES to peace!"

PAUSE 3 SECONDS

Now look into the upper right section of the mirror and see the reflection that is now forming there. Visualize a group of young families. There are husbands with their wives. Some of the wives are holding babies. There are other children holding onto their parents' hands. See them. Imagine them. These are happy families who will spend many years with each other in love and joy. This section of the peace mirror is called "The Right To Love."

Now mentally repeat this phrase with me as I say it. I love peace, and I want peace for everyone, forever. I say YES to peace!"

Now take your green crayon and write the word YES in bold letters across this reflection in the mirror.

PAUSE 5 SECONDS

Now I want you to say out loud this same phrase with me as I say it again. "I love peace, and I want peace for everyone, forever. I say YES to peace!"

PAUSE 3 SECONDS

Now look into the lower left section of the mirror and see the reflection that is now forming there. Visualize a large conference table. In the center of the table is a globe of the world. Sitting on the table next to the globe is a replica of the Statue of Liberty. The leaders of all nations are sitting around the table. They are talking and smiling. They are discussing how to solve problems to everyone's satisfaction. They are sharing their knowledge and resources. See some shake hands as they reach agreements. See this scene. Imagine it. These are the powerful leaders of the world making sure that peace endures for everyone forever. This section of the peace mirror is called "Peaceful Solutions."

Now mentally repeat this phrase with me as I say it. "I love peace, and I want peace for everyone, forever. I say YES to peace!"

Now take your green crayon and write the word YES in bold letters across this reflection in the peace mirror.

PAUSE 5 SECONDS

Now I want you to say out loud this same phrase with me as I say it again. "I love peace, and I want peace for everyone, forever. I say YES to peace!"

PAUSE 3 SECONDS

Now look into the lower right section of the peace mirror and see the reflection that is now forming there. Visualize a group of merchants. They are selling domestic goods. Men, women and children are purchasing food, household furnishings, toys, clothing and other domestic items at reasonable prices. They pay the merchants a fair price, and they receive value for their money. Everyone is smiling and happy. See this scene. Imagine it. These are people enjoying the fruits of their labor. This section of the peace mirror is called "Peaceful Prosperity."

Now mentally repeat this phrase with me as I say it. "I love peace, and I want peace for everyone, forever. I say YES to peace!"

Now take the green crayon and write the word YES in bold letters across this reflection in the mirror.

PAUSE 5 SECONDS

Now I want you to say out loud this same phrase with me as I say it again. "I love peace, and I want peace for everyone, forever. I say YES to peace!"

PAUSE 3 SECONDS

You have now examined four of the many beautiful aspects of peace. Peace gives "Freedom from Fear." Peace gives "The Right to Love." Peace seeks "Peaceful Solutions" to problems. Peace gives birth to "Peaceful Prosperity" for everyone.

You have now examined war and renounced it and destroyed it in your consciousness. You have examined peace and strengthened it in your consciousness.

The power of your thoughts has become part of mass consciousness. Thus you have influenced mass consciousness to embrace peace more and war less. This is good, and this is so.

Every time you listen to this tape, you will go ten times deeper than before and your thoughts will be ten times more effective than before.

If you listen to this tape twice a month, that is good. If you listen once a week, that is very good. If you listen once a day, that is excellent. I recommend that you strive for excellence. The more often you use this tape, the greater influence you have on mass consciousness for the cause of World Peace.

In a few moments I will count from one to five. When I reach five, open your eyes. You will be wide awake and feeling fine.

One . . . two . . . three . . . coming up slowly now. Four . . . five . . . open eyes, wide awake, feeling fine.

● ● ●

World Peace

(Tape Two)

WITH THIS tape you will greatly expand your influence on mass consciousness for the cause of World Peace.

You will enter into a state of relaxation where you will be more effective in projecting your thoughts and energies.

World Peace
Tape Script Two

Close your eyes.

Take a deep breath and slowly exhale as you begin to relax.

I want you to imagine now that you are looking at a clear, blue summer sky. In the sky, a skywriting airplane is writing your first name in white, fluffy, cloudlike letters. See your first name in the sky, white fluffy, cloudlike.

PAUSE 3 SECONDS

Now let your name just drift away. Let the wind just blow your name away into the blue. Forget about your name. Forget you even have a name. Names are not important. Just go on listening to my voice as you relax and go deeper with every breath you exhale.

I want you to imagine now that you are standing on the top step of a heavy wooden spiral staircase. Feel the carpet under your feet. The carpet can be any kind and color you wish—create it.

PAUSE 3 SECONDS

Now extend your hand out and touch the railing. Feel the smooth polished wood of the railing under your hand. You are standing just ten steps up from the floor below. The stairs are curving very smoothly down to the floor below. In a moment we will walk down the stairs. By the time you reach the floor below you will be deeper than you have ever gone before. Take a step down now, down to the ninth step smoothly and easily. Feel yourself going deeper. Now down to eight, deeper still. Now down to seven . . . six . . . five . . . four . . . three . . . two . . . one. Now you are standing on the floor below. There is a door in front of you. Reach out and open the door. From the room beyond the door a flood of light comes streaming out through the open doorway. Walk into the room, into the light through the open door. You are inside the room now, look around you. This is your room, and it can be anything you want it to be. Any size, any shape, any colors. You can have anything in this room that you want. You can add things, remove things, rearrange things. You can have any kind of furniture, fixtures, paintings, windows, carpets, or whatever you want because this is your place—your very own private inner place and you are free here. Free to create, free to be who you are. You are free to invite anyone you wish into this room and communicate with them. You are free to do whatever you will, and the light that shines in this room is your light. Feel the light all around you, shining on the beautiful things in your room. Shining on you; feel the energy in the light. Let the light flow all through your body now. Going in through every pore in your skin. Filling you completely. Pushing away all doubt. Pushing out all fear and tension. You are filled with the light. You are clear and radiant, glowing with the shining light in your room.

Here in your room, your consciousness is in perfect harmony and communication with mass consciousness. Whatever you think in this room, whatever you say in this room, and whatever you do in this room will make a significant impression on mass consciousness.

While you are in the light in your room, I want you to make a commitment to support World Peace with all the mental and spiritual energy you can generate. Say the following words to yourself with me as I say them: "I love peace, and I want world peace for everyone, forever. I impress my desire for world peace on mass consciousness for action."

PAUSE 3 SECONDS

Now I want you to repeat those same words out loud as I say them. "I love peace, and I want world peace for everyone, forever. I impress my desire for world peace on mass consciousness for action."

PAUSE 3 SECONDS

There is a chair in the center of your room. Sit in it.

PAUSE 3 SECONDS

There is a button on each arm of the chair. If you press either button, your mirror of peace will descend from above and be in front of you. Press one of the buttons now.

PAUSE 5 SECONDS

Your mirror of peace has now descended and is in front of you. Take a few moments now to study the mirror. It is the size of a movie screen. It has a gold frame around it with a name plate at the top that says "Peace."

There are four reflections in your peace mirror. Study them.

PAUSE 5 SECONDS

In the upper left section there are people of all cultures mingling on a city street. They are happy and free. They have freedom from fear because their world is at peace. Study this scene. Imagine it. Absorb the harmony and love from it.

PAUSE 5 SECONDS

Now mentally say the following words with me as I say them. "I want freedom from fear for everyone. I direct mass consciousness to achieve this."

Now repeat these same words out loud as I say them. "I want freedom from fear for everyone. I direct mass consciousness to achieve this."

PAUSE 3 SECONDS

Direct your attention now to the reflection in the upper right section of your peace mirror. There are families together having an enjoyable time—fathers, mothers, children. All are happy to be with each other. Study this scene. Imagine it. Absorb the love and security from it.

PAUSE 5 SECONDS

Now mentally say the following words with me as I say them. "I want everyone to live in love and harmony. I direct mass consciousness to achieve this."

Now repeat these same words out loud as I say them. "I want everyone to live in love and harmony. I direct mass consciousness to achieve this."

PAUSE 5 SECONDS

Direct your attention now to the reflection in the lower left section of your peace mirror. See the world leaders there working in cooperation with each other to maintain world peace. They are happy and sincere. A replica of the Statue of Liberty is there also as a symbol of world peace. Study this scene. Imagine it. Absorb the power and unselfishness from it.

PAUSE 5 SECONDS

Now mentally repeat the following words with me as I say them: "I want world leaders who are dedicated to world peace. I direct mass consciousness to achieve this."

Now repeat these same words out loud as I say them. "I want world leaders who are dedicated to world peace. I direct mass consciousness to achieve this."

PAUSE 5 SECONDS

Direct your attention now to the reflection in the lower right section of your peace mirror. See merchants and customers engaging in commerce. The merchants are getting fair prices for their peacetime goods. The customers are getting good value for their money. Everyone is smiling and happy. There is no greed. There is no cheating. There is only honest exchange of goods and money. Study this scene. Imagine it. Absorb the confidence and sense of well-being from it.

PAUSE 5 SECONDS

Now mentally say the following words with me as I say them. "I want a world economy that is based on peace and on honest dealings. I direct mass consciousness to achieve this."

Now repeat these same words out loud as I say them. "I want a world economy that is based on peace and on honest dealings. I direct mass consciousness to achieve this."

PAUSE 5 SECONDS

In a few moments I will stop talking for five minutes. I want you to stay in your room and do whatever you wish for world peace until I begin talking again. For instance, you may want to invite someone into your room and tell them that you want them to become dedicated to world peace and to do whatever they can to make world peace possible. You may want to visualize scenes in your gold mirror that depict what peace means to you and then release those scenes to higher consciousness for action. You may want to make affirmations about world peace such as you have already done during these tape sessions. Your affirmations may be out loud, they may be mental, they may be visual. What you do now is your own personal contribution to influence mass consciousness however you wish to do so. I will now stop talking for five minutes.

PAUSE FIVE MINUTES
while the tape continues to run

You have now made a significant contribution toward influencing mass consciousness for World Peace.

Every time you listen to this tape, you will go ten times deeper than before and your thoughts will be ten times more effective than before.

If you listen to this tape twice a month, that is good. If you listen once a week, that is very good. If you listen once a day, that is excellent. I recommend that you strive for excellence. The more often you use this tape, the greater influence you have on mass consciousness.

In a few moments I will count from one to five. When I reach five, open your eyes. You will be wide awake and feeling fine.

1 . . . 2 . . . 3 . . . coming up slowly now. 4 . . . 5 . . . open eyes, wide awake, feeling fine.

● ● ●

Hypnosis for Beginners
Reach New Levels of Awareness & Achievement
William W. Hewitt

Hypnosis is one of the most valuable tools available for the enrichment of lives. It's a normal, safe, healthy phenomenon that brings you to the altered state of consciousness needed for directing your mind to specific goals. The power and scope of self-hypnosis can blow your mind into new, heightened levels of awareness and achievement.

When you are finished with this step-by-step guide, you will be able to hypnotize yourself and others safely and easily. Whether your goal is to stop smoking, control migraine headaches, or commune with your spirit guides, you will find hypnosis routines that you can use for any purpose, including special tips for hypnosis with children. In addition, you will be able to record your own audiotapes to regress yourself into past lives. Several case histories from the author's own clientele dramatically illustrate the power of this remarkably simple yet profound technique.

1-56718-359-X, 5³/₁₆ x 8, 288 pp., softcover   **$9.95**

To order, call 1-877-NEW-WRLD
Prices subject to change without notice